T0272730

Mark Wheeller

Can't Believe
I'm Saying This
To My Mum!

Contemporary Duologues

Salamander Street

PLAYS

This edition first published in 2020 by Salamander Street Ltd.,
272 Bath Street, Glasgow, G2 4JR (info@salamanderstreet.com)

Can't Believe I'm Saying This To My Mum!
© Mark Wheeller, 2020

Extracts from *'I Love You, Mum – I Promise I Won't Die'* (2019), reprinted with
permission of Methuen Drama, an imprint of Bloomsbury Publishing Plc.Extracts
from *Scratching the Surface* (2016), *This Is For You* (2020) and *Can You Hear Me Major
Tom?* (2020), reprinted with permission of Pping Publishing. Extracts from *Kill Jill*
reprinted with permission of Maverick Plays and Musicals for their Australasian
market. Extracts from *Sequinned Suits to Platform Boots* reprinted with permission of
Maverick Plays and Musicals. Extracts from *Butcher, Butcher Burning Bright* reprinted
with permission of Oxford University Press.

PB ISBN: 9781913630621
E ISBN: 9781913630614

10 9 8 7 6 5 4 3 2 1

Further copies of this publication can be purchased from
www.salamanderstreet.com

CONTENTS

Acknowledgements

To all those (as named in the verbatim duologues) for offering their words to make my plays as truthful as memory will allow. Without them none of this would be possible.

Rachael, and my family, who encourage my commitment to writing these plays.

My Mum and Dad for support/encouragement all through my life.

David Bowie for opening my eyes and ears!

Roy Nevitt for inspiration as a young YT director to see that there was more to productions than a glitzy musical!

The members of Stantonbury /Epping/Oaklands/Oasis/ Birmingham Rep/Romsey Community Youth Theatres, Alderbrook School, Beaumont School & The Victoria Shanghai Academy who put so much work into premiering the plays these duologues come from to give them such a solid start in life!

Equally, Ape, StopWatch, TiEitUp Theatre Companies have also been central in making a name for my plays and offering me the opportunity to watch them develop with a professional company & directors.

I should also thank the many schools/youth theatres who have subsequently worked on these plays and offered them an ongoing platform. Danny Sturrock for his multimedia work/web site input, videography, all of which have propelled my work into this century.

The adult team (Amy Barnett, Kat Chivers, Paul Ibbott, Dave Jones, Richard Long, Matt Sturrock & Chris Webb) at Oasis Youth Theatre/ RSCoYT who added in a variety of ways consistent artistry to my more simple efforts.

Profound thanks to George Spender and those in the Salamander Street team for taking my ideas and running (fast) with them.

Sophie Gorell Barnes and all at MBA for their continued support and belief.

Introduction

I have, for a long time, wanted to produce a collection of monologues from my plays because I know they work well for young performers (and probably older ones as well!). I have granted requests for them to be used in compilations of other such books so, it seemed I wasn't the only one to think they were worthy of such a collection but my previous publisher (Zinc) chose not to go with the idea. Once I started on my *Act Normal* book, my daughter, Daisy, said:

"Dad, you should also include some duologues…"

…and so… following a positive response from George & his team at Salamander Street – one book became two!

Zoom/Social distance friendly performances.

Compiled at a time when social distancing is a consideration, these duologues all lend themselves to this form of working. My advice to you if you think they don't… be imaginative and remember: necessity is the mother of invention. There will be a way!

Young people as performers and the age of each role

I suggest that ALL of these duologues are possible for young people to perform despite the implied age of the person they are playing. Without exception, these extracts were all written for young people to perform. There are some that are specifically teenage characters but, I would not restrict any prospective performers to those. I have seen incredible young performers doing all (bar *Sibling Saviours* which has never been seen) of the scenes in this volume. The age of the performer should be no barrier.

Gender & racial background

What I have said regarding age refers equally to gender and racial background. I have, throughout my lifetime as a Youth Theatre director, blind cast without realising that term or that I'm doing it. I have always cast people with reference to availability, enthusiasm and commitment. The verbatim scenes, in particular, are suitable for gender and racially blind casting because the actor is simply putting their silhouette over the words and should never aim for impersonation.

A note about performance in verbatim/documentary plays

I wrote this paragraph when introducing some of my early verbatim plays and it feel it's appropriate to repeat it here:

It must, at all times, be remembered when reading or performing this play (these monologues), that the events portrayed are as close to the truth as memory allows. The performers should not impersonate the real-life characters, but breathe into them a life that offers a reasonable interpretation of the words. The actors should avoid overstatement (unless otherwise instructed) and veer towards underplaying. You can trust the material… you really can. It is after all as near as possible to the 'real thing'.

My introductions to each duologue

I made a decision to repeat some instructions rather than include them as a generic introduction at the start of the book because, when I have used books like this, I have picked a scene and read the specific introduction to that one alone. So, advance apologies to anyone who chooses to read the separate introductions like a novel… they will be repetitive!

The position of the audience

Many of my plays are not performed 'end on'. They are often in the round or immersive. I have mentioned when they are specifically written to be performed in this way. It makes for a far more interesting monologue to (re) consider where your audience might be. You may also want to change that relationship with the audience as part of the performance of the monologue.

The book title

It was my son Charlie's idea to use a line from one of the duologues as the title for this book. *"What I think is key is that it doesn't sound like you (the writer) talking to the reader through this title, 'helping them to be better actors'. It should be one of your characters reaching out and telling them their story that, in turn, they want to tell themselves."*

The book title was selected from a group of drama teachers from Drama Matters, who saw my shortlist, all of which were lines from the duologues included in this volume. Thanks to all who voted in the poll. **Can't Believe I'm Saying This To My Mum** was a clear winner, which made things easy for me… but do you know which extract it comes from and what the original context was? The answer does appear in the book when this duologue appears. Keep your eyes peeled!

Sequencing the duologues

I decided simply to order the duologues in the order the plays or musicals they derive from were originally written.

Finally...

It is a catchphrase that anyone who has worked with me will be familiar with. Enjoy your work on these. Embark on them *for the fun of doing them seriously*. Let there be much laughter as you prepare together with a determined focus to do as well as you can. Surprise your teacher, your friends, your family, your audience and last but not least, yourself!

Mark Wheeller, August 2020

Blackout – Operation Pied Piper (1983)

ANNE. THOMAS. Serious.

Blackout – Operation Pied Piper *is my large cast musical about the World War II evacuation of children. The British Government code named it* ***Operation Pied Piper***. *My mum (Jean) was evacuated during the war and the story is loosely based around her experiences. The duologue is a naturalistic exchange between the Tom and Anne Reid, who have taken Jean in as an evacuee. Tom and Anne are Jean's second billets, after she and her first ones didn't get on. She has settled well, however, Jean's mother has been killed in the London bombings. Her father, following an awkward visit where he and Jean seemed more like strangers, has decided she must return home. This scene begins with Anne putting the finishing touches to packing Jean's things in preparation for her journey home. Tom accepts the responsibility of having to take Jean to the train station to travel home (alone – not unusual back then). Anne struggles with the idea of losing Jean, who has become like a daughter to her and a sister to their own child, Doreen. This scene should be punctuated by awkward silences full of subtext. Try to imagine what isn't said as well as what is. How does Tom really feel? This is a highly charged duologue. Use the symbols of both the suitcase and the gas mask to add to the intensity of the situation.*

You may wish to cross reference with the monologue book where you can see Tom's way of dealing with saying goodbye to Jean in his final monologue from this musical. The original EBYT production of ***Blackout*** *is available to watch (for free) on YouTube.*

***

*(**ANNE** is packing **JEAN's** things in a suitcase. She finds her gas mask and looks at it. **Tom** enters. Silence.)*

ANNE: Why, Tom? Why now?

TOM: You knew, as well as I did, she would have to go if that's what her father wanted. You've said yourself… she needs to be with her father.

ANNE: She should have stayed until the end of the war. A short visit to London would have been sufficient. Beingthere will only remind the poor child of her mother. I know she was getting over it. He doesn't seem to care how Jeannie feels, how messed about she feels.

TOM: He is her father. We must stand back and let them carry on with their lives.

ANNE: 'Their lives'? She wanted to be part of our life. She said so to me. She told me that. She's part of our lives and she always will be.

TOM: We have to think of our family now.
(Silence.)

ANNE: She's not safe in London. You must see that Tom. *(Silence.)*
It's not right to take her back, a young girl like that.

TOM: We have Doreen. Imagine how she's feeling. She must...

ANNE: *(Not registering.)* She needs me and I need her. Doreen needs her. The farm needs her. It won't seem right here without her.

TOM: We have to accept it, Anne.

ANNE: We have things that we can offer her here, that he can't. It's better for her here.

TOM: Anne! He needs her now. You seem to forget. She is his daughter. *(More calmly.)* Isn't it better that they're together?

ANNE: I'm sorry. You think I'm being silly.

TOM: No. I know exactly how... well...

ANNE: When she goes... Tom, I don't think I can bear to see her again. Not ever. I just...

TOM: Oh come on now.

ANNE: I just won't be able to.

TOM: We don't have to decide that now.

ANNE: I know, but I want you to know that's...

*(**TOM** moves to comfort **ANNE**. She breaks away from him to speak.)*

Would you take her to the train to... I don't think I could manage it.

TOM: Of course I will.

ANNE: I'll take her bed down while you're out. Doreen said she wanted it done as soon as possible.

Silence. **TOM** *exits, taking the suitcase.* **ANNE** *sits on the bed and puts her head in her hands.*

Graham – World's Fastest Blind Runner (1984)

GRAHAM. MARK. Serious.

Graham – World's Fastest Blind Runner is my play about the world champion blind athlete, Graham Salmon. This is the opening scene setting up the whole (true) story. The scene deals with Graham's death through my memories of phone calls between us and our final meeting… though little did I know that this was the case. Despite the phone conversation being naturalistic, there are opportunities for more stylistic physicalisation from this point onwards:

Mark tries to reach Graham. On each of his lines Mark approaches a new barrier.

*This is an opportunity to outwardly (physically) express my (Mark's) desire to reach Graham. The 'barriers' can be actual or imagined. The duologue includes two brief direct address monologues. At these points, it is important that, the person playing Mark should meet the eyes of the audience (not just one person). Do not fix your eyes above their heads. It needs to be personal and 'direct'. The words become a narrative 'voice over' as though in the present, looking back, while the performer's actions re-live the scene as a visual representation of the images in Mark's mind. It is as though the characters are in two time zones, Graham back in 1999 and Mark in the present day. Mark returns to 1999 (I call this theatrical time travel) for the phone conversations. A crucial decision you will need to make is how you represent Graham's passing. Note: Graham has a line after he dies. I suggest you understate it, making it quiet and gentle. Graham can be involved in gentle acting throughout the final monologue. Again, that's your decision… or he could look on from his resting place, or even turn away and face the back as though not there. OYT's production of **Graham** is available on DVD via Salamander Street.*

***

GRAHAM: (*On the phone*) Mark! Guess what?

MARK: What?

GRAHAM: Guess!

MARK: You won the British Open?

GRAHAM: Better!

MARK: Can't be!

GRAHAM: It is! I got a hole in one!

MARK: *(Laughing.)* Seriously? In the British Open?

GRAHAM: Amazing eh?

MARK: At this point I should tell you that my friend Graham Salmon was totally blind, pretty much from birth.

GRAHAM: And I've just been down the bookies and got amazing odds on doing it again.

MARK: *(Laughing.)* Typical!

I met Graham in 1982 when, along with a team of actors from the Epping Youth Theatre, I wrote a play telling of his athletic achievements. After that, Graham and I developed a lasting friendship. I was proud to have him as my Best Man when I married and, with Marie *(Pronounced Mahrie.)* his wife, they proved wonderful godparents to our children.

(Laughing.) I remember Graham taking up golf a few years after retiring from athletics. Most people learn the basics with a friend and then get professional help… not Graham.

GRAHAM: No… get professional help straight away!

MARK: It epitomised his approach. Within a year he was in the British team!

GRAHAM: *(To the audience.)* The year after that, mine was the first name on the team sheet!

MARK: I used to call him; 'Storybook Man'. His life was full of exciting achievements…

(Changing the pace.) Unfortunately my 'Storybook Man' was equally acquainted with tragedy. Cancer, which caused his blindness as a baby, struck again just a year after the hole in one:

GRAHAM: *(Speaking into a phone.)* Mark. I have some very grave news.

MARK: I remember him saying "grave" and thinking it wasn't a "Graham" word at all.

GRAHAM: They've discovered a tumour in my thigh. In the muscle.

MARK: What's gonna happen?

GRAHAM: They're taking my leg away.

MARK: *(Indicates the line of the amputation on his own body.)* He was to have a hindquarters amputation, a rare and unpleasant operation...

GRAHAM: ... and five weeks in hospital.

MARK: The nurses loved him and were amazed by his determination to walk. Things seemed to be improving then, following a holiday, there was another call and they had to come home early.

GRAHAM: My other leg's swollen up.

(MARK tries to reach GRAHAM. On each of his lines MARK approaches a new barrier.)

MARK: It was so difficult to know what to say...

GRAHAM: The cancer's back and they've found nodules in my lungs.

MARK: Can't they do anything?

MARIE: The doctor says it's terminal.

GRAHAM: I just want some extra time. Extra time with Marie.

MARK: He battled for another year, desperate to enjoy Christmas and see in the millennium but...

GRAHAM: It wasn't to be. *(Perhaps he turns to face the back.)*

MARK: He died in terrible pain in October 1999. Graham is the most inspiring person I can ever meet. He...

GRAHAM: *(Turning back with energy.)* ... represented Great Britain in every major athletics competition between 1977 and 1987.

MARK: Ski'd in the Winter Olympics.

GRAHAM: Played cricket at Lord's

MARK: Ran the London Marathon...

GRAHAM: … and for a while held the British High Jump record for the blind!

MARK: A few weeks before he passed away, my two boys and I visited him at his home. Although I was shocked by how the harsh regime of steroids had transformed his athletic appearance, I was delighted to witness his remarkable spirit was very much alive, even in this most difficult period. We were talking when suddenly, my six year old Charlie, said, and bear in mind Graham had just had his leg amputated:

'Will you come out and play football?'

I shouldn't have been surprised… Graham agreed and, supported by crutches, swung his good leg at the ball taking shots. My boys were impressed by how many times he scored! As the pain became too much, he sat in his wheelchair and did headers.

That spirit had always been there. In fact, his parents had seen it pretty much from the start.

Too Much Punch For Judy (1987)

JUDY. JO. Serious.

Too Much Punch For Judy is my verbatim play telling the true story of Judy, who killed her elder sister, Jo, in a tragic drink driving incident. Judy was the driver (in her sister's car – trying to protect her from a second drink drive conviction) and her sister was the passenger. When this collection came to be made this was the first duologue I thought to include. I frequently used it to encourage my students to add unrelated movement (i.e. decorating) to the duologue, but to see how underlying action was altered to highlight a content point or change of pace. This is a verbatim account from Judy, remembering what Jo had said to her. One line, in the middle of the naturalistic duologue sees Judy time travelling into 'now time' to narrate her thoughts to the audience. This speech is direct address. As such, it is important that you should meet the eyes of the audience at large (not just one person). Do not fix your eyes above their heads. Jo remains back in the 1980s for this paragraph, with Judy imperceptibly joining her there as they move into live action dialogue – I call this theatrical time travel. She remains there for the remainder of the naturalistic conversation where the audience are not included. OYT's production of **Too Much Punch For Judy** *is available on DVD via Salamander Street.*

***

JUDY: I'll tell you something that is really weird. It was really strange. We were in her new flat doing some decorating and she said:

JO: I think I'll make a will.

JUDY: Joanna! You think of the most funny things! What on earth do you want to make a will for?

JO: I just feel that I should. I mean if anything happens to me now I've got the flat, there could be quite a bit of money involved and I'd want your Leanne to have it.

JUDY: What? You can't be serious.

JO: Well, you don't know this… but Denise did my Tarot cards… twice… and I got the death one… both times.

JUDY: Joanna! You shouldn't mess around with things like that. I'd never go into Denise's house, let alone do that! It's like the Evil Dead house. Really creepy!

JO: Don't be stupid! What can happen to you?

JUDY: If I pulled it out, that'd be it! I'd be so frightened. I'd be like the Doomsday book, walking around, wondering when it's going to happen.

JO: You're being silly! Denise told me it doesn't necessarily mean that you, personally are going to die; it could mean the death of a relationship.

JUDY: Aren't you scared?

JO: No. Why? Should I be? *(Silence.)*

JUDY: *(To the audience.)* One week later we had the accident. *(Pause.)* The Monday before the accident I gets this phone call from Jo. *(Yawning.)* It was about five or six o'clock in the morning…

JO: It's me.

JUDY: What the hell do you want?

JO: Can you come and pick me up?

JUDY: Where are you?

JO: Saffron Walden police station.

JUDY: What've you done?

JO: Got stopped for drinking and driving and they won't let me drive my car home 'cos I'm still over the limit and I've got to get to work.

JUDY: Okay. I'll come and get you. Stay where you are. I went over there, took her to work and took her back to get her car in the evening. She didn't seem too bothered about it really. "What on earth are you going to do? How are you going to get to work if you're banned?"

JO: I dunno. I'll have to think of a way round it when I've been to court.

JUDY: Well, there's not a lot of transport from Dunmow to Epping, is there?

JO: Don't worry! Alison goes into Epping at about the same time, she'll give me a lift. I'll get round it somehow… it's not your problem so don't worry!

JUDY: How much had you had to drink?

JO: Just the usual.

JUDY: Yeh?

JO: Some wine. Not a lot.

JUDY: Don't you see! You'll be banned! I bet you were well over the limit!

JO: Judy! You're more worried about it than I am! Look! I don't want anyone else to know. I want you to promise me you won't tell Mum. *(Pause.)* You know what she's like; it'll make her worry and it's not necessary.

JUDY: Okay then.

JO: I want you to promise.

JUDY: I won't tell Mum. I promise.

(They freeze. Silence.)

Hard to Swallow (1989)

JOHN. MAUREEN. Serious.

*Hard to Swallow is my play telling the true story of Catherine Dunbar, who died after a long battle with anorexia. This is a documentary play (as opposed to verbatim) as it was developed from Maureen Dunbar's book, **Catherine.** This scene focuses on an example of arguments in the family home over Catherine's eating preferences and shows her parents' different attitudes towards them. The duologue is naturalistic and should be performed as though you are 'in the moment'. Maureen's final speech sees her time travelling into 'now' time, to narrate her thoughts to the audience. This speech becomes direct address. As such, it is important that you should meet the eyes of the audience (not just one person). Do not fix your eyes above their heads. It needs to be personal and 'direct'. John remains back in the 1970s throughout the scene. OYT & Romsey School's production of **Hard to Swallow** is available as a double bill on DVD via Salamander Street.*

***

JOHN: She knows the rules. She'll eat when and where she's told to. If not, she needs to be punished!

MAUREEN: John, she's not well.

JOHN: I insist she eats with us.

MAUREEN: It'll only make matters worse.

JOHN: Can't you see if she goes on getting her own way things will get even worse?
*(**JOHN** goes to exit as if to retrieve **CATHERINE.**)*

MAUREEN: You don't understand! The school have sent her home because they think that she hasn't eaten anything for nearly two weeks.

JOHN: *(Incredulous.)* Two weeks?

MAUREEN: That's what the school have told me.

JOHN: And what does Catherine have to say?

MAUREEN: She says it hurts when she swallows.

JOHN: Why didn't you tell me?

MAUREEN: I was going to… later on.

JOHN: Well, we'd better do something about it.

MAUREEN: The school have advised me to contact a psychiatrist.

JOHN: A psychiatrist?

MAUREEN: Catherine needs help.

JOHN: Not that kind!

MAUREEN: She thinks she's fat.

JOHN: She's not!

MAUREEN: But she thinks she is.

JOHN: How can she be fat if she hasn't eaten for two weeks? It doesn't make sense.

MAUREEN: That's why she needs to see a psychiatrist.

JOHN: She needs to be sat down at our table and made to eat.

MAUREEN: She's agreed to eat, so long as we allow her to eat on her own. Does it really matter where she eats?

JOHN: Yes it does! Of course it does!

MAUREEN: As far as I'm concerned she can eat every meal alone, so long as she does eat!

JOHN: She will eat with us in our dining room and there will be no more arguments!

MAUREEN: It's not as simple as that.

JOHN: It is! Simon and Anna eat with us so why can't Catherine? We will not pander to her.

MAUREEN: John, please… trust me… just this once.

(Silence.)

JOHN: Maureen, I am the head of this family and therefore I am the one who makes decisions.

MAUREEN: Be it on your own head. *(Pause.)*

Even when he dragged her back to the table she would secretly place her food in her pockets and little, if any, was ever consumed.
One week later she was admitted to hospital having lost more and more weight every day.

Hard to Swallow (2)

CATHERINE. ANNA. Serious.

__Hard to Swallow__ is my play telling the true story of Catherine Dunbar, who died after a long battle with anorexia. This is a documentary play (as opposed to verbatim) as it was developed from Maureen Dunbar's book, __Catherine.__ This scene focuses on an example of arguments in the family home over Catherine's anorexia and how it affected the sibling relationship. The duologue is naturalistic and should be performed with the characters being 'in the moment'. Catherine's opening speech is from her diary but remains in the 1980s, so the performer will have to decide if it is appropriate for her to perform the speech as direct address, meeting the eyes of the audience. There is ample opportunity to portray outward emotion in this scene. It is not underplayed as I have suggested in many other duologues in this volume. This offers an opportunity to 'let go'!

You will possibly choose to use real props (a suitcase full of pill bottles) for this scene as well as Catherine's diary. OYT & Romsey School's production of __Hard to Swallow__ is available as a double bill on DVD via Salamander Street.

***

CATHERINE: 26 February 1983: Without Mummy I am totally unable to cope.

I dread and fear Daddy's reaction, his fury, frustration and anger because of my inability to be away from Mummy. I am so filled with pain that I don't feel like eating. I am like a new-born infant but with more feeling, fear and loneliness. At night I binge to try and numb my pain and torture myself. Anna is being a little hard on me. If only she could understand. *(Saying her thoughts aloud purposely, so that **ANNA** hears her as she approaches.)* Where are my scales? I am sure that Anna has taken them.

*(She approaches **ANNA** who is asleep and jogs her aggressively.)*

CATHERINE: Anna! Anna, wake up!

ANNA: What do you want?

CATHERINE: I want to know where you have put my scales.

ANNA: I haven't touched your stupid scales. What would I want with them?

CATHERINE: I need to know where my scales are. I know you hid them!

ANNA: Okay, so I did!

CATHERINE: You wouldn't dare do this if Mummy and Daddy were here. You've no right to touch them.

ANNA: You've no right to be in my room!

CATHERINE: Tell me where they are Anna! *(Grabbing her violently.)* I need to see how much I weigh!

ANNA: You know how much you bloody weigh! Your obsession is ruining all our lives! And what's more, I know that you've begun hoarding tablets again. What are you trying to do? You've got enough to kill you four times over.

CATHERINE: I don't know what you're talking about.

ANNA: Alright, if you won't admit it, I'll show you!

*(She runs to **CATHERINE**'s room.)*

CATHERINE: *(Running to the case and clutching it.)* You don't understand. They are helping me to get better. You don't want me to go on like this forever, do you?

ANNA: Won't you ever face up to the truth!

CATHERINE: Go away! Leave me in peace. I know what I am doing.

ANNA: So that's why they had to put you in a psychiatric hospital, isn't it? *(Fighting to get the case.)* Give it to me! *(In the struggle the case is opened and a vast number of medical bottles fall out.)*

CATHERINE: Get out! *(Pushes **ANNA** away with great strength.)*

ANNA: I can't stand you when you're like this! I hate being your sister!

CATHERINE: You'll regret saying that, Anna... you'll regret it.

Sweet (W)FA/Lethal In The Box (1991)

SUE. ROB. Serious.

*Sweet (W)FA (or **Lethal In The Box** in its full-length musical form – Music and Lyrics by Brian Price) is my verbatim play/musical telling the true story of Sarah Stanbury (aka Sedge), an ex-student of mine, whose ambition was to play football (soccer) for England. Her mother (Sue) and the football authorities, back in the late 1980s, had different ideas. This is a naturalistic duologue from Rob and Sue, Sarah's parents. In creating this scene I met with both Rob and Sue and recorded an interview. I asked them to remember the kind of conversations they had regarding Sedge's enthusiasm for football. This was one such memory and I would have returned home and added as much as was needed to their verbatim memories, then returned to ask them to check and correct my script. This is the opening scene in the play and firmly establishes the differing attitudes of Sedge's parents. There is ample opportunity to portray outward emotion in this scene. It is not underplayed as I have suggested in some other duologues in this volume. This offers an opportunity to 'let go'!*

It is a scene that I felt right from the off needed to be in this book as it is so direct and clear with each person in the scene holding such different views. You may wish to cross reference with the monologue book where you can see one of Sedge's teachers, Miss Vallas' view on Sedge's reaction to her interests.

***

A radio is playing in the background … perhaps a football commentary. Sue is doing the housework. Rob is reading the sports pages of a newspaper with half an ear to the after match comments to a Southampton (a.k.a. Saints) F.C. football match.

SUE: Rob … (**ROB** *continues reading.* **SUE** *goes to the radio and turns it off.*) Rob!

ROB: I was listening to that!

SUE: I know!

ROB: What's up now?

SUE: We did discuss it.

ROB: What?

SUE: Don't pretend you don't know.

ROB: I don't know what you want me to say.

SUE: I want you to tell her that she can't wear it.

ROB: I can't!

SUE: We discussed it! We agreed. A football kit isn't right.

ROB: I agreed the pedal car was a good idea.

SUE: You must have put them up to it.

ROB: That's not true.

SUE: Well, why did they get it?

ROB: Sedge probably asked them.

SUE: Why do you call her that?

ROB: Sue! Everyone does!

SUE: Her names Sarah!

ROB: Everyone calls her Sedge. She…

SUE: You think it's one big joke don't you?

ROB: I don't understand what the big problem is.

SUE: If we let her go on like this we'll pay for it, you mark my words. She'll be trouble if we go on like this.

ROB: Like what?

SUE: Rob, she's a girl, a three-year-old girl for crying out loud! How do you think I feel? All the other little girls at playgroup come in after their birthdays showing off their new dresses or new dolls while Sarah struts around in her new football kit.

ROB: But she loves it!

SUE: It's embarrassing! All the other mums are looking at me and thinking… well I don't know what they must think!

ROB: Does it matter?

SUE: Yes! It does! We spent a lot of money on that pedal car to make up for her not having the kit. That should have been the end of it!

ROB: Can't you see Sue, even with the pedal car, she's not happy unless she's getting it to skid!

SUE: And who taught her to do that I wonder?

ROB: She found out for herself.

SUE: You treat her like a boy! What'll it be next? A pint of lager down the club with her mates?

ROB: I just follow what appears to interest her.

SUE: I hope you'll be just as keen when she starts to do things all the other little girls do.

ROB: She loves that kit.

SUE: She looks like a boy!

ROB: She looks great in it. Next month she'll be on to something else. You know what kids are like!

SUE: I hope so, 'cos then I'll throw it away!

Chicken! (1992)

TAMMY. CHRIS. Comic.

Chicken! *is my Theatre in Education road safety play for older people to perform to Key Stage 2. Chris causes the death of his cousin, Tammy, by daring her to cross the road in front of an oncoming vehicle. He manages to keep his part in her death a terrible secret. This scene appears early on in the play, just after the two cousins receive their new bikes as Christmas presents. The two characters often move the action of the play forward by using rhyming couplets. It adds rhythm and comedy to the presentation. These couplets are delivered as direct address, although they can also address comments to the other character. With their direct address it is important that they should meet the eyes of the audience (not just one person). Do not fix your eyes above their heads. It needs to be 'direct'. They are 'in the moment' and the events referred to happen in the present. The scene is used to show the differences between the two characters. Each performer should think what characteristic elements they should bring to the fore in what needs to be a larger-than-life presentation required of this style. The original* ***Chicken!*** *performances were in the round. It may be an idea for you to bear that in mind when presenting this extract. The professional production of* ***Chicken!*** *performed by StopWatch Theatre Company is available from Salamander Street.*

***

TAMMY: *(Wearing a bike helmet.)* Christmas afternoon, we both arrange to meet.

TAMMY & CHRIS: *(CHRIS enters, also wearing helmet.)* "On yer bike at three o'clock at the bottom of the street."

CHRIS: *(Impersonating.)* "You'll miss the Queen do her speech!" me mum she says to me.
So, just to please her, I stay to watch it, then leave at ten past three.
(Impersonating.) "Now wrap up warm… don't want you to catch a chill …
And keep that cycle helmet on!" … "Yes Mum, course I will!"
But once her back is turned… I pull it off my head *(He does.)* …
It's alright… I won't fall off… I won't come back dead!!!

TAMMY: What kept you Chris… no, don't tell me… your mum made you watch the Queen.

CHRIS: Don't be stupid… I was…er… giving my bike a clean.

TAMMY: *(Noticing the bike.)* New bike?

CHRIS: *(Noticing* **TAMMY***'s bike.)* New bike?

TAMMY: Blatantly!

CHRIS: Cool!

TAMMY: Sweet! So… why were you cleaning it?

CHRIS: Well, you know Aunt Ermintrude?

TAMMY: My favourite old Aunt…

TAMMY & CHRIS: … with the knitting needles and the squeaky voice!

CHRIS: Yeah, well, I had to find some use for the home-made jumper she sent me.

TAMMY: Another one!

CHRIS: Yeah, this year it was yellow… with *(Inaudible.)* Winnie the Pooh sewn onto it.

TAMMY: With what?

CHRIS: Winnie the Pooh!

TAMMY: Nice! You'll never guess what she sent me?

CHRIS: I don't know… something cool.

TAMMY: A new iPhone!

CHRIS: I don't believe it!

TAMMY: I can just imagine your mum… "Ooh, isn't that smart. I know… you can wear that when you go to see Uncle Ray and Tammy on Boxing Day. Ooh! I will be proud!"

CHRIS: I've even got to write a thank you letter… that's probably why she keeps sending them… She thinks I like them.

TAMMY: Tell her what a loverly colour it is… "Yellow… ooh! Loverly!" Vomit or what!

CHRIS: Hey, Tammy! Swap?

TAMMY: No way!

CHRIS: Worth a try!

TAMMY: Not really!

CHRIS: Come on… let's go to the park?

TAMMY: Whatever!

CHRIS: I'm not racing!

TAMMY: Didn't say you had to!

CHRIS: You were going to!

TAMMY: What are you on?

CHRIS: My new bike!

TAMMY: Funny!

TAMMY & CHRIS: *(Miming a bike ride.)* Riding to the park we see some mates from school

CHRIS: They can't believe the bikes we're on…

TAMMY: … then Chris shouts out …

CHRIS: Yo, dude!

TAMMY: Uncool!

CHRIS: Riding to the park, I think I'll do some tricks.
A wheelie, an endo and a double flick

TAMMY: Whack on the brakes and do a skid
"Chris has anybody told you you're a real sad kid!"

CHRIS: Yeah. *(Getting off imaginary bikes.)* But I'm changing! Today is not only Christmas Day… today is a turning point in my life. *(He starts to take on superhero persona.)*

TAMMY: A what?

CHRIS: The dawning of a new era.

TAMMY: What?

CHRIS: Hey you! I am a mean machine.

TAMMY: More like a micro machine!

CHRIS: Shut-up!! I'm where it's at… I am where it's happening… Christopher "super-hero" Simpson!

TAMMY: More like Christopher Robin with your friend Winnie the Pooh! *(Reminding him of jumper.)*

Chicken! (2)

TAMMY. RAY. Serious.

Chicken! *is my Theatre in Education road safety play for older people to perform to Key Stage 2. Chris causes the death of his cousin, Tammy by daring her to cross the road in-front of an oncoming vehicle. He manages to keep his part in her death a terrible secret. This scene, featuring Tammy and her father, Ray, is unrelated to the central action of the play but provides a powerful moment where, when I've seen it performed, generates an audible gasp from the audience following Tammy's final line. Tammy introduces the action of the play by using rhyming couplets. This should add rhythm and pace to the presentation and sets the audience up for a dramatic twist to follow. These lines are delivered as direct address. It is important you should meet the eyes of the audience (not just one person). Do not fix your eyes above their heads. It needs to be 'direct'. Once into the duologue, the characters are 'in the moment'. Ray arrives home very worried about Tammy's lateness. Tammy is taken by surprise, as she thinks her father has only just returned home from work. Gradually she catches up and accelerates towards the confidence to deliver her final sting of a line! The gradual status switch should be charted between the two characters as the scene progresses. The original* ***Chicken!*** *performances were in the round. It may be an idea for you to bear that in mind when presenting this extract. The professional production of* ***Chicken!*** *performed by StopWatch Theatre Company is available from Salamander Street. You will hear the reaction from the audience at the end of this scene!*

***

TAMMY: I said goodnight to Gary at the corner of the street.
The front room light's on... Dad's still up... I walk in... all discrete. *(Enters.)*
What?! Dad's not in... what a relief... I thought I'd get loads of grief.
At least he didn't have to wait... he'll have no idea that I was late.

RAY: *(Entering, exasperated.)* I've been out looking for you!

TAMMY: What?

RAY: *(Looking at his watch.)* Ten past eleven... you said you'd be back by ten thirty.

TAMMY: It's only just after.

RAY: I rang your phone but you didn't answer.

TAMMY: It was on silent!

RAY: Anyway it doesn't take you an hour to get home from school.

TAMMY: *(With a wry grin.)* It did tonight!

RAY: I want to know where you've been, what you've been up to?

TAMMY: I haven't been "up to" anything!

RAY: I'm not stupid! You must have been doing something.

TAMMY: Gary walked me home… I don't know… we were chatting.

RAY: Chatting! Tammy. For over an hour! I've been really worried. I've phoned the school and there was no one there.

TAMMY: Dad?

RAY: Don't you "dad" me! Anything could have happened!

TAMMY: Whatever!

RAY: If you hadn't got back by midnight I was going to phone the police.

TAMMY: You often get home later than you say and I don't go phoning your office or telling the police.

RAY: That's different.

TAMMY: It's not!

RAY: If I stay on at work, it's to get enough money to make our lives more comfortable… and you know that!

TAMMY: But you're never here!

RAY: That's not the point… and it's not true! If you want to be treated like an adult you've…

RAY & TAMMY: *(Interrupting.)* … got to behave like one.

RAY: I wouldn't push it if I were you.

TAMMY: I'm off to bed.

RAY: Right! If that's all you've got to say, I'm going to ground you for the rest of the week …

TAMMY: No way!

RAY: And I'm not prepared to discuss it!

TAMMY: But Gary and me are going to the fair on Friday.

RAY: No, you *were* going to the fair.

TAMMY: Dad!

RAY: I can't imagine his parents'll be too happy about tonight either.

TAMMY: They won't mind… they probably won't even be in!

RAY: I'm not having this Tammy.

TAMMY: You're just jealous! *(Immediately regrets saying this.)*

RAY: What do you mean?

TAMMY: Oh, it doesn't matter.

RAY: It does.

TAMMY: I'm going to bed.

RAY: Tammy! You said something. You can go to bed when you tell me what you mean.

TAMMY: *(Pause.)* You're just jealous 'cos you haven't got anybody. I'm sorry Dad, but it's true. *(Exits.)*

Legal Weapon (1996)

ANDY. JAZZ. Serious.

Legal Weapon is my part verbatim play telling the true story of 'Andy's' car accident, framed within a fictional love triangle. Andy's words (relating to the various road traffic incidents and the events in prison) are verbatim. The opening narration is delivered by the performers who go on to multi-role as Jazz (J) & Andy (A). This narration is delivered as a direct address. You should meet the eyes of the audience (not just one person). Do not fix your eyes above their heads. It needs to be 'direct'. The two characters start this scene with a different goal. Andy has to tell Jazz that he has killed her best friend. Jazz has to tell Andy that she has had an affair (with Matt, a character who will interrupt this scene shortly after this extract finishes) and that she is calling off their relationship. Neither is aware of the other's intention but that proves central to the impetus of your approach to each of their performances. Andy communicates his news first, which pressures Jazz to keep quiet about hers, but it will still be there in her mind as her intention, knowing she has promised Matt that it will happen and that he might arrive soon. These different intentions should create an electricity in the scene and affect the way in which the two characters are played and relate to one another. This is a scene I adored watching students perform when I was a teacher. Likewise, when Ape Theatre (professional) Company performed it… it was always a potent scene!

The ability to snap from being a narrator to being a character is a challenge. The scene must change suddenly and come alive after the introductory rhyming lines.

***

J: Both Andy and Jazz have facts to reveal before the end…

A: He to explain he killed her best friend…

J: She to tell him that their bubble's now burst…

BOTH: What words will they summon, and who…

A: Andy…

BOTH: … or…

J: … Jazz…

BOTH: … will dare to tell first?

*(They spring into action becoming '**ANDY** and **JAZZ**'. **ANDY** enters, carrying sports bag in one hand, He arrives in **JAZZ***'s room where a tape plays quietly throughout scene, starting here.)*

ANDY: Am I glad to see you? *(Goes to hug her.)*

JAZZ: *(Holding him at arm's length and looking at his cut face.)* You're cut?

ANDY: I know.

JAZZ: Been in a fight?

ANDY: Not yet.

JAZZ: What do you mean?

ANDY: *(Moving away from her, goes down on his knees to unzip his bag and takes out a bottle of wine.)* Got a corkscrew?

JAZZ: I don't know. *(Starts to look half-heartedly, for a corkscrew.)* Actually Andy, *(Takes the wine and puts it back in **ANDY***'s bag) I don't want to drink and I don't really think you should either.

ANDY: What?

JAZZ: When you phoned this afternoon, I dropped my plans for tonight.

ANDY: What?

JAZZ: I've got a life here Andy!

ANDY: That makes me feel a whole lot better… 'cos me… I'm in trouble, I mean real major trouble.

*(**JAZZ***'s mobile rings. She goes to pick it up.)*

JAZZ: *(She stops the call.)* I'll get it later…

ANDY: No… take it… don't mind me… you've got your 'life' to lead!

JAZZ: I want you to tell me what's happened… it's only Kell.

(Pause.)

ANDY: Who?

JAZZ: Kelly… MacFarlane?

ANDY: It can't be!

JAZZ: Look! *(Shows the phone to him.)*

ANDY: Someone's got her phone then.

JAZZ: What?

ANDY: It won't be her.

JAZZ: It is. I'll call her back if you want.

ANDY: Don't! She… Jazz, that's why I'm here.

JAZZ: What're you on about?

ANDY: It's… it's seriously dreadful news Jazz.

JAZZ: What do you mean?

ANDY: She's been killed. She was on her moped.

JAZZ: Kelly?

ANDY: Yesterday.

JAZZ: Who was that on the phone then?

ANDY: I don't know.

JAZZ: Let me call her back…

ANDY: No, *(Grabbing for the phone.)* don't! Please Jazz… don't…

JAZZ: Why not?

ANDY: Just don't!

JAZZ: Why are you being like this?

ANDY: Please? Listen!

JAZZ: I want to speak to whoever's got her phone. I want to know what's happened! I want to know what's going on!

ANDY: What will you do when you've found out?

JAZZ: I don't know but I've got to do something. She's my mate Andy!

(Pause.) If what you're saying is true it's so unfair cos she was really starting to sort her life out. When did you hear about it?

ANDY: I was there.

(Silence.)

JAZZ: What?

ANDY: That's what I've come to tell you. It was me.

JAZZ: No!

ANDY: She pulled out without looking. I didn't know it was Kelly till last night. That's why I needed to tell you in person. I'm so sorry Jazz.

(Silence.)

JAZZ: When did this happen?

ANDY: Yesterday. in the afternoon...

JAZZ: Where?

ANDY: Vortisore Lane.

JAZZ: Behind our old school?

ANDY: *(Nods in agreement.)* She just pulled out of the garage without looking!

*(Message alert tone sounds... **ANDY** tries to grab the mobile but **JAZZ** keeps it.)*

JAZZ: What're you doing? *(Calling the answering service.)* It's Kelly again... a voicemail. Kelly never leaves voicemails. *(**JAZZ** dials voicemail.)* It's Kelly's mum. *(She listens to the message and updates him with sporadic comments as **ANDY** paces.)* She's phoning all the numbers on Kelly's phone to let us know... oh shit Andy! The funeral's next Tuesday. *(For the first time on the edge of tears.)* They're saying it wasn't her fault? *(Puts the phone down.)*

What the fuck have you done? Do they know it was you?

ANDY: They're saying I was speeding.

JAZZ: Were you?

ANDY: I didn't think I was.

JAZZ: Who says you were then?

ANDY: Accident Investigation Unit.

JAZZ: Were you or weren't you? Why are they saying it? How do they know?

ANDY: They do these tests. I had to sit and watch. They drive along the road at forty, and then brake where my skids began. They keep doing it... going faster and faster until finally the car reaches the point where I...

JAZZ: How fast?

ANDY: You don't want to know.

JAZZ: Tell me Andy!

ANDY: They're saying seventy... but I'm sure I wasn't... I'm certain!

JAZZ: You fucking idiot! *(Pause.)*

ANDY: I won't argue with that.

JAZZ: *(More detached.)* How did you get here?

ANDY: What?

JAZZ: Please tell me you came by train.

ANDY: No.

JAZZ: You drove?

ANDY: Can't you be more understanding?

JAZZ: You killed my mate and you want me to be 'more understanding'?

  (Silence.)

Remember how you felt when your Grandad died. You wanted those kids locked up! You wanted the key thrown away! I can hear you say it!

ANDY: They were robbing him! They were breaking the law!

JAZZ: So were you!

ANDY: They'd done it before!

JAZZ: So have you! Loads of times!

ANDY: Jazz, please…

JAZZ: I want you to go!

ANDY: I need you to help me.

JAZZ: I can't. Not now, not after this!

ANDY: You've got to.

JAZZ: I can't even look at you without thinking what you've done… we're finished Andy.

ANDY: Don't say that Jazz.

JAZZ: She was my mate!

(Silence.)

Parents or... Do As I Say (1997)

TOM. CAZ. Serio-comic.

*This scene was written at around the time of **Legal Weapon**, when Road Safety Officers were discovering the power of Drama as a tool for educating young people about road safety. This scene was produced as part of a Drama teaching pack for schools (in Essex I think). It is a self-contained scene and one that I took out of the teaching pack context and used frequently in my Drama/Theatre teaching. Until this collection it has never been available outside my own school. It is short and easy to access for young people, allowing an opportunity for gentle conflict. I used it to encourage my students (normally in Key Stage 3) to add unrelated movement (i.e. sorting out the business of drinks and using the catalogue) in respect of the spoken content of the duologue and explore how that action can be add a natural context for the scene. Tom has an intention from the start which drives his part in the conversation. Caz's intention is less clear but, as we discover in the last line, she has one too, and the way in which the outcome is negotiated through this conversation is neat!*
The scene is entirely naturalistic. The status relationship between the two characters is interesting as it shifts at times.

***

CAZ, *aged about thirty-five, enters and takes off her coat, puts the kettle on to make a cup of tea. Her eighteen-year-old son,* **TOM**, *is in the kitchen sitting at the table flicking through a catalogue.*

TOM: What did you get Mum?

CAZ: Don't ask!

TOM: That bad eh?

CAZ: Worse!

TOM: Come on. What happened?

CAZ: *(Opening a cupboard.)* I don't believe it! No tea bags.

TOM: *(Going to the fridge.)* Here's a lager. *(Gives the can to* **CAZ**.*)*

CAZ:	Thanks.
TOM:	You got a ban didn't you.
CAZ:	And the rest! *(She opens the can.)* Six months and a two hundred pound fine.
TOM:	Told you would. You wouldn't believe me.
CAZ:	It wasn't as if I was drunk… no one got hurt.
TOM:	What are you going to do about work?
CAZ:	Will you stop quizzing me!
TOM:	It's just that… well I was thinking… I could drive you.
CAZ:	And then have my car. I can see right through you Tom. You think "Right, Mum's banned so now I can have her car." Well you can't! Let's get that sorted from the start!
TOM:	You've got no use for it!
CAZ:	I might have to sell it to pay the fine.
TOM:	You can pay that by instalments. Come on! Why don't you want me to drive it?
CAZ:	Because I don't trust you! (**TOM** *gives* **CAZ** *a knowing look.*) Oh I don't know Tom. *(Pause.)* I ain't got much option really have I?
TOM:	Excellent! Thanks Mum! Don't worry, I won't be as bad as Dad, and you let him drive it!
CAZ:	He used to frighten me to death.
TOM:	It used to be like going to school in a roller-coaster.

CAZ:	And he never got caught! I don't want you pulling any of his tricks in my car.
TOM:	I know… *(Mimicking)* … "Do as I say, not as I do" then I'll be okay!
CAZ:	I'll ignore that!

(Pause.)

TOM:	Mum?
CAZ:	Yeh.
TOM:	Can I use the car tonight? It's just that… well…
CAZ:	Tom!
TOM:	Well I couldn't ask you yesterday because… you know.
CAZ:	You had this all planned didn't you? What if I said no?
TOM:	You won't, I know you won't!
CAZ:	Where are you going?
TOM:	I'll be careful.
CAZ:	Where are you going?
TOM:	I had a phone call… you know from the Rose and Crown.
CAZ:	You've got a job.
TOM:	Barman.
CAZ:	I'm done for drink driving, you're offered a job in a pub and you want to borrow my car to get there. I must be mad!

TOM: *(Pointedly.)* Yeh but I don't drink and drive. Anyway I'll pay the petrol.

CAZ: Too damn right you will! Oh in for a penny, in for a pound, but one condition.

TOM: What's then?

CAZ: Drinks for me... on the house.

TOM: How are you going to get there? You haven't got a car.

CAZ: No. *(To the audience.)* I don't need one any more. *(Laughs.)* I've got a chauffeur!

The Most Absurd (Promenade) Xmas Musical In The World... Ever! (1997)

ALAN. BIANCA. Comic.

The Most Absurd (Promenade) Xmas Musical In The World...
Ever! *is my musical (with music by James Holmes) telling an absurd story of a fairy tale land (The Bower of Bliss, stolen from* **Wacky Soap***) where a new fairy tale star is born and identified by a gift for composing music. The King and Queen employ two secret agents to discover and kidnap this person, leading to her parents wanting to keep her identity a secret. It transpired she also has the power to save Xmas but, as that doesn't affect this scene I won't go into that! The musical was written to be my hit Xmas musical. Thus far this hasn't happened, though when we performed it in Southampton on two different occasions it went down a storm... and one school also performed it very successfully in the middle of summer to be even more absurd! This scene occurs at the point where Bianca (the future fairy tale star) has just written the song that will save Xmas and where her parents (father in this slightly adapted version) have a 'great' idea about how to disguise her. It is wonderfully mad and owes more than a nod to Monty Python, who I loved as a teenager. The story is surreal and the delivery of both characters must be 'over the top'/exaggerated wherever possible – and even with the 'not-possible', try to make it so! You should perform the scene with a huge sense of fun! I am so pleased to be able to include this scene here, as it's one I loved directing, and would have loved to perform in it as a student!*
The original performance was in promenade style. The action took place amongst the audience. It may be an idea to do this in your presentation. It makes the whole experience far more immersive and visceral.

***

ALAN: I have an idea to get us out of this mess! I will speak to Bianca when I next see...

BIANCA: *(Entering excitedly.)* Dad! Quick! Come into the conservatory! I've just composed an amazing tune and it will make a wonderful Xmas song, if only I could find a talented lyricist.

ALAN: Bianca, there's something I need say to you actually.

BIANCA: Quick then, because I need to play this tune to you. It's the best one I've ever, EVER composed!

ALAN: Sit down sweetheart!

BIANCA: *(She remains standing.)* Why? What's going on?

ALAN: Bianca? Your mother wants me to talk to you.

BIANCA: Go one then.

ALAN: We have decided to… decided to…

BIANCA: Decided to what?

ALAN: But I don't know how to tell you?

BIANCA: Take a deep breath and spit it out. It can't be that bad!

ALAN: Bianca, please sit down … please. *(**BIANCA** sits down.)*

ALAN: No stand up. *(She does.)* No, sit down.

BIANCA: I'll sit … *(Sitting.)* but I want you to tell me… whatever it is!

ALAN: *(Deep breath.)* We need you to wear a disguise.

BIANCA: A what?

ALAN: We have decided you must dress you up as a … as a…

BIANCA: Dad?

ALAN: As a cactus!

BIANCA: You're winding me up!

ALAN: Not a spiky one but a rubbery one.

BIANCA: You are winding me up!

ALAN: I'm not!

BIANCA: You are… now will you come and…

ALAN: Bianca! Listen to me and don't interrupt!

BIANCA: Ooooooh! Don't be so oppressive. I'm only a small child. Now, draw a big breath Daddy and tell me what you want to say MUCH MORE CALMLY!

ALAN: *(Deep breath.)* We can't risk anyone suspecting that you are the infamous fairy-tale character with the gift of music because, if they do, we know that they will kidnap you!

BIANCA: And me walking around dressed up as a cactus will stop everyone from suspecting will it?

ALAN: I don't want an argument about it!

BIANCA: *(Standing.)* I don't want to be a frigging cactus!

ALAN: This is my house and while you're living under my roof, you'll do what I say.

BIANCA: Can't you just go out and lose me in the woods like they used to in the olden days? *(Sits stroppily.)*

ALAN: I wish it were that simple, but it isn't. And there's something else, Bianca.

BIANCA: What?

ALAN: I think you'd better sit down.

BIANCA: *(Standing… in a rage.)* I am sitting down!

ALAN: If I say you'd better sit down… then… then you must be standing up… so… put your bum on the chair and sit yourself down right now, pin your ears back and listen to what I have to say. *(**BIANCA** sits.)*

BIANCA: Just get on with it!

ALAN: Right! *(Deep breath.)* We can't allow you to compose any more music.

BIANCA: You can't do this to me!

ALAN: Oh yes we can! I haven't told you the complete truth. Earlier this evening Special Agents… really silly Special Agents visited us. They were searching for you. We managed to dupe them into taking your doll but…

BIANCA: My doll? My…

ALAN: They wanted you… look…

BIANCA: But I love my doll.

ALAN: … and we love you. Look Bianca… we are trying to protect you.

BIANCA: You're the Baddies… far worse than any goblins or witches I've ever read about …

ALAN: You could be in prison now if it weren't for …

BIANCA: I'd rather be in prison than… well at least I could play my music there and I wouldn't have to dress up as… as a cactus!

SLEEPING: I think you'll look very… well… you'll look just like a cactus!

BIANCA: I don't want to look like a cactus!

ALAN: Well… how about a Pantomime cow?

BIANCA: That might be better, but …

ALAN: I've got it!!! When alone in the house, you can dress normally and play your music quietly but when we go out or if we have any visitors, you will be the back of a pantomime cow. I'll talk to nanny. She can be the front. *(Aside.)* That'll shut her up too!

BIANCA: Okay then. As long as I can compose my music!

ALAN: That's decided! Now, I'll tell your mother you've agreed… finally… and then I suggest we all get ready for Xmas. *(He exits.)*

BIANCA: Can I play you my song? I'll close the windows and sing it quietly! *(He has ignored her and left.)* Why does no one ever listen to me? *(She puts her head in her hands and slumps in her seat and cries.)*

Missing Dan Nolan (2002)

PAULINE. GREG. Serious.

*Missing Dan Nolan is my verbatim play telling of the tragic circumstances surrounding the disappearance of Dan Nolan from Hamble, Hampshire in January 2002. This scene was developed from a recording I made of Pauline (and Greg) telling me their fears regarding the whereabouts of Dan, prior to the discovery of his remains. It was the first time in my life I'd heard the term sex trafficking. I remember thinking how this seemed such an alien idea. Only six years later, I was writing a play about human trafficking and realised it was happening more than I could ever have imagined… and closer (geographically). An utterly awful realisation for me, I can only imagine how it must have been for the Nolan family. I wrote the scene using ideas turned into dialogue from the words they said into my tape recorder. I returned to them to check over what I had done. I remember this was one of the few occasions where they wanted to make some corrections which, of course, were duly interpolated into this scene. Not until the final ten lines should this scene be delivered by direct address. At this point the performers should turn to face the audience and meet the eyes of the audience (not just one person). Do not fix your eyes above their heads. It needs to be personal and 'direct'. The earlier parts of the scene are presented naturalistically as though it is a live conversation, 'in the moment'. You may decide to add a physical context (as I talked about in the previous duologue). For example, Greg could be busy doing something unrelated, when he is interrupted by Pauline's out-loud thinking. It could be anything but it gives the scene a context/setting. Pauline may have been in the middle of doing something else, so may have an unrelated prop with her. Do give this setting some thought to ground it in their everyday reality. The thoughts in this speech are heart-breaking for any parent and so, at times, Pauline will be expressing her emotions openly while Greg tries to calm her, without dismissing or belittling her incredibly worrying (to him as well) thoughts. OYT & Litchfield Garrick YT's production of **Missing Dan Nolan** is available as a double bill on DVD via Salamander Street.*

***

PAULINE: Greg… I was talking to this chap in Cowes today. *(Silence.)* He lost his daughter. *(Silence.)* It's a frightening thought. *(Silence.)* Greg… he told me that kids in Eastern European countries were being sold… sold for sex. Dan could have been abducted. He could have been down there and gone aboard a boat, or got in a car…

GREG: Pauline… don't…

PAULINE: We know that other teenage boys had been targeted… we know they were, so he could've been.

GREG: You're just upsetting yourself.

PAULINE: I want to figure out what happened.

GREG: I know.

PAULINE: And it… it could go on like this forever.

GREG: We've got to face it.

PAULINE: But you know what really upsets me… it's that no one was there with him. If someone had been there, it would almost certainly have reduced the chances of him being abducted. No one was there to raise the alarm. No one was there to witness if he had gone in the river. No one was there to help him. He was on his own. That was probably the first mistake he'd made… in his life.

GREG: He was such a good lad. I don't mean goodie-goodie, I mean…

PAULINE: I know exactly what you mean…

GREG: It's just not fair…

PAULINE: I want to… no, I… I need to know what he went through.

GREG: Pauline… there may never be a conclusion.

PAULINE: There's got to be.

GREG: We may never know what it is. That's what I can't accept… can't get to grips with. *(Silence)*

PAULINE: Why Dan? It doesn't seem real.

GREG: Life'll never be the same.

PAULINE: So many people walk such a fine line…

GREG: … and they survive.

PAULINE: We've been privileged… blessed to've had a son like Dan…

GREG: Such a special boy, anyone who knew him will tell you that.

PAULINE: A very much-loved son… who has brought us so much joy and laughter.

GREG: A son truly to be proud of.

PAULINE: We will always miss him.

GREG: We are missing him dreadfully.

The Gate Escape (2003)

COREY. SUE. Stylised/serious.

The Gate Escape is my part-verbatim play telling the true story of various school truants framed within a fictional Big Brother (TV reality show) framework. That framework is not relevant in this extract. It is a duologue I use a lot in my teaching, both at my own school (when I was a teacher) and when I am out delivering practical workshops. It is a great example of a 'Two Touch' or 'Précis Theatre' scene from the moment when Corey's stylised argument with her mum begins. This is also the duologue from which the title of this volume comes. The scene starts off with a direct address (verbatim) monologue from the teenage Corey. As such, it is important that, as a performer, the person playing Corey should meet the eyes of the audience (not just one person). Do not fix your eyes above their heads. This needs to be personal and 'direct'. The words become a narrative 'voice over' as though in the present, looking back, which leads Corey to travel back in time to re-enact a scene with Sue, her mum. The 'live action' scene needs to click in with no fuss. Suddenly, Cory is 'in the moment' with Sue. She imperceptibly returns back into direct address mode at later points in the scene. The Two Touch section, starting 'Then the arguments began…' is followed by a clear performers' direction which indicates the sudden change in style. 'State the lines as though they are lines from the argument in the style that is described and building to a climax.' For example, the performer should say the line 'Taking up from the last time…' as though that is what they are doing. They can indicate this by vocal inflection and physicalisation/gesture. This is a scene where I find teenagers are able to more fully understand 'stylisation'. Enjoy working with this scene. I am confident my students did. A well performed version of Corey and Sue's argument can be seen in isolation on the **Wheellerplays The Author's Definitive Collection** *DVD via Salamander Street. It would be very helpful to illustrate this performance style to students who are unfamiliar with it.*

***

COREY: At Easter of Year 8 I started going out with this guy who was fifteen. Billy went to a different school, well, *(Chuckling.)* I don't think he 'went' much at all. I met him at the park. We just got talking and it was, well, I'd nicked sweets before but this was something else. He was nicking all the time; make-up, CDs, clothes. It got to the point where people'd give us a list of what to get for them. We'd get about £200 worth of stuff a day and sell it on for about £30! Who says money doesn't grow on trees? I could buy loads of fags and not be paying for them.

One week, in October, I was in Year 9, we bunked off for three days in a row. That's when Mum got involved…

SUE: Corey?

COREY: What have I done now?

SUE: Have you been to school today?

COREY: Course!

SUE: So why did Mr Biscuit phone up and say you weren't there?

COREY: Mr Biscuit is an idiot. You know he is. He sent me to the Medical room with Jenny… she'd had a nosebleed. He probably forgot…

SUE: Well he could have phoned to let me know…

COREY: He said he would…

SUE: Well he didn't… I've a good mind to go up to that school and…

COREY: Don't worry Mum… he's a prat… everyone knows he is! Fortunately, she never asked what was in my bag…

SUE: So… what is in your bag then?

COREY: Mum!!!

SUE: Only joking…

COREY: It was jam-packed full of stolen stuff!

SUE: Well if you do ever bunk… you'll be grounded.

COREY: Everyone says my writing's like my mum's… so I forged notes… another little crime to add to my list!

SUE: Suspecting what was going on, I went into school and gave them a different signature…

COREY: The next day, when I went to hand my note in… the one I'd written… saying I'd had a doctor's appointment…they said: "That's not your mum's signature. Your mum brought us a copy of her… her new signature… look…"

I got an hour's detention... but it did nothing to stop me from bunking.

SUE: Then the arguments started...

COREY: *(As though arguing, stating the lines as though they are lines from the argument in the style that is described and building to a climax.)* Ongoing...

SUE: Taking up from the last time...

COREY: ... bringing stuff up from the past...

SUE: ... clutching at straws...

COREY: ... Lying...

SUE: ... suspecting...

COREY: ... but not proving...

SUE: ... not being able to prove anything...

COREY: ... provoking...

SUE: ... feeling frustrated...

COREY: ... defensive...

SUE: ... attacking...

COREY: ...shouting...

SUE: ... louder...

COREY: ... hurtful...

SUE: ... passionate...

COREY: ... swearing...

SUE: ... what has happened to you?

COREY: ... bad swearing... can't believe I'm saying this to my mum... really bad swearing...

SUE: We didn't bring you up like this Corey!

COREY: ... tearful...

SUE: … out of control…

COREY: … raising hands…

SUE: … fists…

BOTH: Fighting!

COREY: Then dad got involved…

Kill Jill (2005)

JILL. BECKY. Comic.

Kill Jill, *is my play fusing two stories and one overarching idea. 1/ Tony Martin shot a repeat-offender burglar in the back as he was leaving his property, sparking a huge debate over the rights of property owners. 2/ Jack and the Beanstalk, where the thief is treated with more compassion than the victim. 3/ Reality TV and the morality surrounding non-intervention of those who are filming the 'real' people. I love this play and its conceit, though it is (currently) far less well known than many of the others included in this volume. This is the opening scene and sets the situation up where Jill becomes the 'Reality Star' in the fictional 'Lottery Reality Show'. Her participation in the show comes at a time when her parents have just split, but she has a 'duty to entertainment' to complete her month's 'national service' to entertainment. There are opportunities for absurd humour between the parent and daughter. The performances should use a melodramatic style of performance.*

***

One (or two) chair(s) beside a table with an over-large card saying GONE in big letters. **BECKY** *enters and sees the letter/card. She reads it and slowly moves to sit by the table, head in hands, crying.*

JILL: *(Enters and sees* **BECKY** *is upset.)* Mum? What's the matter? *(She puts her arm round her.)*

BECKY: Don't love… *(Laugh/crying.)* you'll make me cry even more.

JILL: Is it Dad?

BECKY: Yeh.

JILL: He's gone? *(***BECKY** *holds up the card saying GONE.)* For good? *(She turns the card round. It says FOR GOOD.* **BECKY** *cries loudly.)* We'll be okay Mum.

BECKY: I don't know what we're gonna do.

JILL: What do you mean?

BECKY: How'll we cope?

JILL: We will Mum. Don't worry.

BECKY: *(Angrily.)* It's easy for you to say that.

JILL: I didn't mean to be...

BECKY: I know... it's just...

JILL: Do you want me to get you a cup of tea?

BECKY: *(Melodramatically allowing her pent-up emotions to come out.)* Jill! We can't even afford tea bags! *(Pause, then very slowly.)* I only have one quander left.

JILL: *(Brightly.)* I have two quanders... that'll be enough. I'll pop out and get some?

BECKY: This isn't how your opening scene should be... me crying... everything going wrong like this.

JILL: So, we've must do something.

BECKY: Like what?

JILL: Show grit and determination?

BECKY: How?

JILL: Take each other's hands.

BECKY: Look up to the heavens.

BOTH: And vow to overcome whatever problems are put before us.

BECKY: No... that's kak!

JILL: You suggest something then?

BECKY: Wreak revenge on Dad's new girlfriend.

JILL: Mum?

BECKY: No, we can't afford to go wherever it is they've gone!

JILL: Mum? Do I have to do this?

BECKY: What?

JILL: This *Lottery Reality Show* thing?

BECKY: Of course you do!

JILL: Why?

BECKY: It's your duty.

JILL: Duty?

BECKY: Your public duty to entertain.

JILL: But why me?

BECKY: As you know, it could have been anyone… and it will be next month. Anyway you said you wanted to be famous.

JILL: But not like this.

BECKY: You have to think of other people's entertainment Jill.

JILL: It would've been fine last year…

BOTH: … when we were happy?

BECKY: Not much entertainment in a happy family is there?

JILL: No. Suppose not.

BECKY: But there will be if you turn things around and become happy.

JILL: Yeh! You could find a rich boyfriend!

BECKY: I can't… I…

JILL: Don't go making excuses…

BECKY: Well if it's that easy you go and do it!

JILL: Alright. I will.

BECKY: Seriously.

JILL: I like a challenge.

BECKY: What about my tea bags?

JILL: I'm on a mission! *(Hands **BECKY** the coins and exits with determination!)* You get them!

Butcher, Butcher Burning Bright (2006)

STUEEY. IAN. Serious.

Butcher, Butcher Burning Bright *is my Theatre in Education fire safety play for older people to perform to Key Stage 3. It has since become popular with KS3 students to perform/explore. Stueey is obsessed by anything related to fire and becomes involved in a situation which leads to the death of Ian's girlfriend, Molly, after the three of them have broken into their school at night, ostensibly to help Stueey find evidence to contradict an accusation Mr Butcher made about bad-boy Stueey which led to him being permanently excluded. This scene occurs after the school fire has broken out. Ian is getting cold feet and wants to report what happened to the police. Stueey disagrees. Stueey knows more about the fire than Ian. What is exciting about this duologue is that the action of the fight between the two boys is integrated into the conversation/argument they have. It is a challenge to make this appear natural yet believable (and controlled) and which enhances the tension between the two boys, as Ian gradually gains in confidence. Stuueey tries to show that he is still in command of the situation, knowing that the events have run away with themselves and, with that, his control is gradually disappearing. Stueey is actually very worried but is determined not to show it! There is an opportunity for some lively (fighting) action here! Stueey is sitting on Ian pinning him to the floor and holding him roughly by the neck. A well executed version of this scene appears on the* ***Butcher, Butcher Burning Bright*** *DVD by RSCoYT available via Salamander Street.*

***

STUEEY: We didn't do nothing. Right?

IAN: Get off!

STUEEY: Button it!

IAN: Get off!

STUEEY: Say it!

IAN: What?

STUEEY: You won't squeal!

IAN: I won't!

STUEEY: You'd better not!

IAN: *(Gives one last twist to IAN's arm.)* Ow!

STUEEY: *(Getting off and releasing IAN.)* You're dead if you say anything! I mean it!

STUEEY: No one knows we were there.

IAN: Molly?

STUEEY: Apart from Molly.

IAN: You said Shuttle saw you.

STUEEY: Well he didn't!

IAN: You said he did.

STUEEY: He was too busy on his, like go-kart thing!

IAN: What?

STUEEY: When I was outside watching for you, he was, like riding around... real cool.

IAN: What about the CCTV?

STUEEY: We had our hoods up most of the time.

IAN: Let's just go to the old bill and say we were there.

STUEEY: Loser! I can't believe you're saying that Ian.

IAN: But we've got nothing to hide? I mean you even stayed there watching.

STUEEY: I told you, it would've looked much stranger if we'd bailed out. Everyone was standing there looking. I wanted to get on TV and do a sob story about all my course work going up in flames... that would have been a real laugh... *(Mock posh voice.)* "All that effort going up in smoke!" *(He laughs.)* Banging!

> *Pause.*

IAN: Stueey? Those notes... was it you?

STUEEY: Might've been.

IAN: It was, wasn't it?

STUEEY: But I didn't set the fire!

IAN: Why did you write them?

STUEEY: What do you think?

IAN: To scare Butcher?

STUEEY: It was his fault I got excluded.

IAN: And before that. 'Cos there were some before you were kicked out weren't there?

STUEEY: I don't know… I'm not a bloody psychologist!

IAN: Butcher, Butcher Burning bright… Stu… why?

STUEEY: It's like based on an old rhyme…

IAN: Stueey? I didn't torch the school… so, who did?

STUEEY: It could have been anything… an electrical fault… anything could have happened!

IAN: But it didn't, did it?

STUEEY *approaches* IAN. IAN *swings at* STUEEY. STUEEY *catches his punch.*

IAN: You don't scare me any more. Hit me if you want, but it won't do any good! I know you did it… but I won't say anything 'cos I can't prove it.

STUEEY: You say anything and you're dead!

Sequinned Suits and Platform Boots (2006)

SHAKEY. BLOCKBUSTER. Comic.

Sequinned Suits to Platform Boots is my theatrical tribute to Glam Rock, which I described as a play that wanted to be a musical. It is a part biographical fantasy focussing on Shakey Threwer's desire to be the next Glam Rock Star. Shakey has written a Rock Opera about a Monk, who was thrown out of a monastery for getting a nun pregnant! (Yes… that bit was me as a fourteen-year-old. The Monkey's Revolt Rock Opera actually exists… as yet unperformed). This scene shifts into fantasy gear when the superhero, Blockbuster appears before Shakey as a (Jean) Genie to offer Shakey the opportunity to make his dreams come true! This offers an opportunity for absurd humour (which I have always been keen on writing) between the super-hero and real teenager. The performances should use a melodramatic style!

If you have the ability/inclination, there is also the opportunity for an exciting (glamtastic) choreographed entrance by Blockbuster, setting the scene alight from the very beginning!

***

THE BLOCKBUSTER *by The Sweet, accompanied by flashing blue lights and smoke as* **Blockbuster***, (a Glam Rock superhero figure) enters melodramatically. Finally, after short dance, (s)he adopts a commanding position before* **Shakey***.*

SHAKEY: Who the hell are you?

B'BUSTER: *(Speaking in a melodramatic voice.)* The Blockbuster!

SHAKEY: (S)he was actually an incredibly imaginative device to the seemingly impossible problem of getting Chinnichap, the glamtastic record producers to attend *Monkey's Revolt*, the glamtastic Rock opera I had written.

How can you help me?

B'BUSTER: I stole the opening riff and the number one spot, from a small Jean Genie.

SHAKEY: You're speaking in riddles.

B'BUSTER: I'm a Genie.

SHAKEY: So, how does that help me?

B'BUSTER: Along with the riff, which was stolen anyway, I also stole… three wishes!

SHAKEY: Three wishes? Now, this sounds wayyy more interesting.

B'BUSTER: Command me, oh master!

SHAKEY: This can't work… you're just a fictional character!

B'BUSTER: So are you!

SHAKEY: Yes, but within the fiction you're fictional!

B'BUSTER: At least I don't spend half my lines talking to the audience!

SHAKEY: Can you really make wishes come true?

B'BUSTER: Make your wishes fictional 70's teenager and then you'll see.

SHAKEY: I wish Chinnichap would come and see *Monkey's Revolt.*

B'BUSTER: *(Laughing.)* Impossible!

SHAKEY: *(Threatening.)* Grant it or I'll reduce you to a pulp… fiction!
(He indicates in a self-satisfied way to the audience his "cleverness" with words.)

B'BUSTER: I'm only joking! Of course I can grant it. Next!

SHAKEY: Two tickets for David Bowie's Aladdin Sane gig in Bristol this June

B'BUSTER: Granted!

SHAKEY: Bowie was the centre of my universe and had just announced his tour and tickets would be in short supply! So… my final wish!

B'BUSTER: This has to be the biggie! Are you ready to see my extraordinary powers?

SHAKEY: I hope so!

B'BUSTER: Ah, shame. I've got to go! My mum'll be getting worried!

SHAKEY: Your mum?

B'BUSTER: She's really strict! Look, I'll grant it later. *(Preparing to leave in*

the dramatic manner of the entrance with music and lights blaring out.)

SHAKEY: Hold on! Stop! *(The lights and music stop.)* Listen! I wish I was a rock superstar with fans worshipping me and...

B'BUSTER: *(The* **BLOCKBUSTER** *faces* **SHAKEY***.)* I said wishes... not miracles!

SHAKEY: And with that... the Blockbuster left! *(There is loud music,* ***Blockbuster****, and flashing lights as the* **BLOCKBUSTER** *exits in a melodramatic and highly charged manner.)* And I was left to see if he did have the power to make my dreams come true. Hashtag...

SHAKEY & B'BUSTER: neverdoubttheblockbuster!

Sibling Saviours (2008)

BRIAN. SHARON. Comic.

Sibling Saviours, is a self-contained scene which has never, until now, seen the light of day… not even in my own lessons. When this book was mooted I remembered it in some detail and looked it up and am so pleased to release it as an exclusive! In 2008 I was accepted onto John Burgess' amazing Playwriting course at the (old) Nuffield Theatre in Southampton. It was the first time I'd ever had any formal tuition in playwriting. It was an eye-opener and, I feel, developed my work significantly, particularly with reference to structuring plays. Sadly, as a result of pressure from my (then) full-time work, where our School suddenly became an Academy, I was unable to complete the course. I also confess that my failure to impress John, was gnawing away at my self-confidence… but I remain very grateful for what the course did offer me. Thank you, John!

At this point, early on in the course, John was encouraging us to be more pacy in our writing and to try, where possible, to only use words of one syllable. I think he was aiming to get us to extend the range of our writing and for me science fiction was a complete departure! The context of this particular exercise was John asking us to look at the human implications of science in theatrical performances. I have no idea whether he suggested the specific subject (I don't remember knowing anything about sibling saviours before this) but it is an idea that made an indelible impression on me, to the extent that I wrote it in one evening on that course and remembered it clearly these twelve years later! It is a naturalistic scene and has a science fiction feel to it.

***

BRIAN: I don't even like her, Mum!

SHARON: That's not the point!

BRIAN: What is the point then?

SHARON: Doing this for your sister is the reason we had you. *(Pause.)* We love you but it … this is just how it is sweetheart. *(Silence.)* If you weren't here, Jamie would die.

BRIAN: When?

SHARON: We don't know the exact time love but she would. It's a very special responsibility you have Brian and you are the only person able to do this.

BRIAN: But I don't want to.

SHARON: Now you're just being selfish.

BRIAN: But Mum?

SHARON: I'm so glad Jamie can't hear what you're saying. This a good thing you're doing and you should be proud of yourself.

BRIAN: When do we have to leave?

SHARON: When Dad gets back. He and Jamie have gone off to get you something very special. Something very expensive that you've wanted, for a very long time.

BRIAN: What is it… is it…

SHARON: There's no guessing. It will be a surprise. We'll put it in your bag and when you get to the hospital you can have it.

BRIAN: How long will it be til they get back?

SHARON: *(Laughing.)* Any minute now.

BRIAN: I want to see what it is.

SHARON: I suggest you go and play while Mummy gets everything sorted.

BRIAN: *(Turns to leave. Turns back to face **SHARON**.)* Will it hurt Mummy?

SHARON: No. You'll be fast asleep.

BRIAN: What about after?

SHARON: No. You'll have to stay in bed for a while but…

BRIAN: How long?

SHARON: A few days…

BRIAN: Days?

SHARON: … but you'll be asleep for most of that time. Please don't worry.

BRIAN: Could I die?

SHARON: You'll be in the hands of experts.

BRIAN: So it is possible?

SHARON: Anything's possible sweetie. I mean, you could step out onto the road and...

BRIAN: Don't I need my organs?

SHARON: It's all been assessed Brian. By the doctors. They do know what they're talking about.

BRIAN: How come you can't give them yours?

SHARON: Ours won't work as well inside Jamie.

BRIAN: And mine will?

SHARON: Yes. That's why you're her 'sibling saviour'. Sibling means brother or sister and saviour means you have the power to save. You are saving Jamie. It's like your job... and a very important one too!

BRIAN: What happens if Jamie's heart stops working? Do I have to give her my heart Mummy?

Granny and the Wolf (2008)

WANDA (a wolf). BECKY (a wolf). Seriocomic

Granny and the Wolf, is my black comedy re-imagining of the Red Riding Hood story. Granny and the Wolf are engaged in an illicit relationship, unbeknown to either of their families. In this scene, Antonio Wolf has decided to inform his mother. He knows the news is unlikely to go down well but, with his dad away, sees an opportunity for a private revelation. In the play this duologue cuts from this scene to one where Antonio sees Granny after the revelation. I remember being particularly pleased with this when I wrote it, and hope when you work with it you are able to pull out all the inherent drama of the situation, which mirrors so many others in a more real life. It represents the clash of generations and their attitudes. It is a naturalistic scene and should be played for truth with no exaggeration nor wolf impersonations. There can be an indication of wolfness in any costume you choose to use. You will need a squeaky dog toy!

***

WANDA: *(Switching off her mobile phone in anger and talking to herself.)* Good for nothing old rubbish, that's all that comes out of those three little bloody pigs – *(ANTONIO enters, WANDA remains unaware.)* – they should never let them into the courts! Smelly and dirty, nearly as bad as those disgusting, furless, gun toting, good for nothing humans! *(Pause. This last remark hurts ANTONIO. He turns ready to abandon his visit, but stands on a squeaky dog toy drawing attention to himself. WANDA turns in slow motion to look at ANTONIO.)* Antonio?

ANTONIO: Mum. *(He takes his foot off the dog toy. Some dog toys emit a sound when the foot is removed, which can add a further comedy moment.)*

WANDA: My darling! My boy! How wonderful to see you. Where have you been? Let me get you something to eat. If I'd known, why didn't you say? I'd have prepared something special, something nice, you know…

ANTONIO: I've… I can't stay long.

WANDA: It's been three weeks… more. Why the rush now? Your dad, he… he won't be home for a while.

ANTONIO: That's a good thing. We can chat. Just you and me eh?

WANDA: Without your father?

ANTONIO: There's something I need... I want to tell you and... I wouldn't have come in if Dad were here.

WANDA: What do you mean? You came through that door unannounced, no apologies. Now you're implying that your dad...

ANTONIO: ... I've found someone, Mum...

WANDA: Why would that be a problem?

ANTONIO: It's not... not for me. Someone to laugh with all the time, it's...

WANDA: ... that's all we've ever wanted. We want you to be happy... but you just seem to be... I don't understand...

ANTONIO: ... Dad certainly won't...

WANDA: We thought you'd... well we didn't...

ANTONIO: ... I couldn't say anything. I didn't want to upset you. I've always tried to do the right thing.

WANDA: *(Becoming even more forthright.)* Well, it's a funny way of going about things because you're not... not doing the right thing at all! No. So, sit down and listen Antonio. Sit down! *(He does.)* If this creature is so perfect, so wonderful, well, why can't we meet her? It is a "her" isn't it? *(**ANTONIO** nods.)* If she means so much to you, why don't you bring her home? Are we that embarrassing? Is that it? Are you so ashamed that you can't even ...

ANTONIO: ... SHE ISN'T A WOLF!!

*(There's a long pause. **WANDA** turns in slow motion to look at **ANTONIO**. There is a moment where she does not know what to say.)*

WANDA: What?

ANTONIO: She isn't a wolf.

WANDA: What do you mean, 'She isn't a wolf'?

ANTONIO: Mum! I don't want to argue!

WANDA: I want you to tell me what she is... this new 'friend'?

ANTONIO: She's a…

WANDA: … not a fox is she?

ANTONIO: *(Smiling.)* … she can be!

WANDA: This is no time for jokes, Antonio!

ANTONIO: I'm trying to make things easier. Look…

WANDA: … then tell me, tell me who this friend is! I want to be… I want to be happy that you've got a new life and everything's changed… but… *(Pause.)*

ANTONIO: She's a human mum.

WANDA: She's a… *(ANTONIO nods.)* What am I meant to say to that? *(ANTONIO shakes his head.)* How do you think that makes me feel? Your dad will…

ANTONIO: I know and that's why…

WANDA: *(Confronting him angrily.)* We didn't raise you to be a pack-deserting, cutlery using, kitten fearing, little human lover! How do you even trust them?

ANTONIO: You've got them all wrong Mum, they're…

WANDA: … I can't believe you're saying this! They carry axes!

ANTONIO: Don't be so daft!

WANDA: Your dad says they do… I mean… what will he think?

ANTONIO: I can't let him ruin this for me. It's the happiest I've ever been so, if you really want me to be happy, support me.

WANDA: I just want you to come home and for everything to be like when you were young.

ANTONIO: I'm a grown-up Mum! I have my own life and my own opinions. *(He makes to leave.)*

WANDA: You've forgotten everything we've ever done for you.

ANTONIO: I haven't. *(WANDA slowly stands to one side indicating that he should leave. ANTONIO leaves, but before he does he kisses her on the cheek. She remains unresponsive.)* I promise you that. I haven't. *(He exits.)*

WANDA: *(Calling after* **ANTONIO**.*)* I'll have to tell your father, you know that Antonio. We never have secrets. We don't… not ever!

Driven To Distraction (2009)

ZINC. JO. Serious.

Driven To Distraction *is my Theatre in Education road/bus safety play for Key Stage 3/4. This was the fourth commission for a road safety play so, to make it more interesting to me, I put it in the context of someone who had been a band member of someone like Gary Glitter (of whom in the 70s, I was a fan but about whom, appalling revelations were appearing in early 2000s) whose life was impacted because of guilt by association. This back story was superimposed onto a story of a young rap star being killed by a bus driven by Zinc (the former band member), who had been distracted by the anti-social behaviour of passengers picking on someone in the bus who was unable to defend themselves. The two young people in the play (Tabs and Emma) were written by Danny Sturrock (who was very near their age at the time) and the older characters (featured in this extract) by me (who was about their age at the time) to gain distinctive 'voices'. The characters are 'in the moment' throughout this scene. We are thrown into the middle of an unfolding situation. The opening moments of this extract need to be informed by the action leading to it. Zinc was obviously on the phone but what was Joe doing, she was clearly unaware of Zinc being on a phone call? What had made her enter at that moment? What was her (disrupted) intention? This is a decision the performer needs to take before embarking on staging this scene. How will that decision affect Joe's attitude in the scene, particularly at the start? The play was written while on the John Burgess Playwriting course, so a number of things he was pointing out would have been at the forefront of my mind at this time. I was conscious of using mostly one syllable words to make the speeches direct, differentiating the two characters to make them more consistent in their responses throughout the scene and how actions inform portrayal of the characters. This conversation isn't a standard conflict but does feature differing takes on the given situation so, will need a degree of subtlety to convey the scene. There is no clear resolution. I think it is important for the performers to decide what they think the resolution would be, so they have an indication of the relative status of the characters.*

***

ZINC: *(Putting his phone down.)* That was Mike…

JO: *(Entering.)* What was?

ZINC: The phone.

JO: Didn't hear it? Mike from the reality show thing?

ZINC: Yeh. They want an answer by the end of the day.

JO: And?

ZINC: I'm still not sure.

JO: You know what I think?

ZINC: It's just not my kind of thing love…

JO: Then, why haven't you already turned them down?

ZINC: Because I know you want me to do it.

JO: You'd like your name out there again wouldn't you?

ZINC: Not right now.

JO: It's a lot of money. It could end up being a massive amount and lead to other stuff and, at the moment, everyone's on your side.

ZINC: The local press is not 'everyone'!

JO: You're this 'have a go hero'. It might kick start your music again. You'd love that if it did, wouldn't you?!

ZINC: 'If', yeh.

JO: It'll be an opportunity to put your side forward.

ZINC: My side isn't that interesting. I knew nothing about what he was up to! Anyway, these things are edited to max the viewing figures, to make 'good telly'!

JO: You are good telly! Your views on Simon would be for sure!

ZINC: I'd probably say the wrong thing and end up in more trouble!

JO: Look, my parents have bailed us out for the last few months, willingly, but that can't go on forever. I'm doing my management course and that'll lead to something sometime but, we need money now. You have your past. We can trade on that. It's our best chance.

ZINC: I was just a guitarist in a group!

JO: In *Hungry Wolf* for God's sake! Anyway, when Simon left you…

ZINC: But it only got to number eighteen…

JO: It was the first Hungry Wolf song I'd heard, so for me you were the lead singer. I didn't even know about Simon…

ZINC: Careful Jo, you're getting all dewey eyed!

JO: *(Smiling.)* There's no danger of that right now!

(Silence.)

ZINC: Jo?

JO: I didn't mean it like that.

(Pause.)

ZINC: There's something else Mike said that worries me.

JO: What?

ZINC: Simon's likely to be released the week the show goes out.

JO: I thought he was in for life!

ZINC: That's what Mike said.

JO: No wonder they want you. This could be huge, Zed.

ZINC: Yeh but people won't suddenly want to hear our music. If anything it'll turn them off.

JO: You haven't done anything wrong!

ZINC: Yeh, but Simon did! Guilt by association Jo! I mean, why hasn't there ever been any interest in a tribute band?

JO: People'll be intrigued though. They'll want to know what you think!

ZINC: They'll just want me to say how terrible he is. It's not as simple as that, and even that might sound like I'm supporting what he did in some way or avoiding taking a stance on it… or him. I just didn't know what he was up to. He never travelled with us anyway. How could we ever guess what was going on? Look Jo, the bottom line is I don't want it all dragged up again. It seems like it's incriminating to've been in his band! *(Pause.)* I'm really not sure at all!

One Million To STOP THE TRAFFIK (2010)

PHIL/TRAFFICKER. COJO. Serious.

One Million to STOP THE TRAFFIK is my documentary play (as opposed to verbatim, as the dialogue was taken from written materials rather than an interviews), telling various stories of human trafficking. The play also documents STOP THE TRAFFIK'S (the organisation) ground-breaking work to fight human trafficking, at a time when the problem went largely unreported. In this scene (adapted slightly from the one in the play where an ensemble was present too), we see Phil (a key worker in STT), narrating into a scene where a ten-year-old is trafficked from West Africa.

In TIE work, actors are expected to multi-role. Here Phil is expected to play the trafficker as well. The performer will need to differentiate the two characters. This can also be assisted by the simple addition of a costume/prop but there needs to be some alteration to their physicality/voice too. It varies between 'live action' and reflective direct address speech. Remember, with the direct address sections it is important that the performers should meet the eyes of the audience (not just one person). Do not fix your eyes above their heads. Direct address needs to be personal and 'direct'. In this scene I decided to put the direct address in the third person (he/she rather than I/we). This is to more obviously focus the audience's attention on the fact that the performers are not the real people in this scene. They become a commentator on the action and can, in the way they deliver the lines, 'comment' on them using facial expression or voice tone. The body of the performer can still exist in the time their narration is referring to (dual time performing). For example in this section:

PHIL: People placed the bags onto Cojo's head.

COJO: They were so heavy he often fell down.

PHIL, *representing the* **TRAFFICKER,** *can pass to* **COJO** *(who is by now also narrating his own actions) the bag (probably mimed as it would be too heavy) the bag of beans and 'Cojo' sinks to the ground as he narrates the action. My advice about third person work is don't overthink it. The audience will go along with it if you don't draw attention to it by feeling awkward. Act confidently… as well as acting 'normally'! OYT's production of* **STOP THE TRAFFIK** *is available on DVD via Salamander Street.*

***

PHIL: In West Africa boys are trafficked to work on cocoa farms. Agents hang around bus stations looking for children, such as Cojo, *(Indicates him, as he enters.)* who are alone or begging for food.

COJO: I left home to earn money for my family. When I got to Sikasso bus station, I... *(He looks around the bus station.)* ... I knew no one.

TRAFFIKER: What is your name?

COJO: Cojo Sir.

TRAFFIKER: Looking for work Cojo?

COJO: Yes.

TRAFFIKER: I take you to my brother.

COJO: He has work?

TRAFFIKER: Yes. The Ivory Coast.

COJO: I have come to work in Sikasso. My father has died. I must stay near my mother.

TRAFFIKER: Work here pays badly. Cojo, come with me to Korgho.

COJO: Here?

TRAFFIKER: No, but you will make lots of money.

COJO: Thank you sir but I stay here to work.

TRAFFIKER: My brother pays very well. Will be good for your poor mother?

COJO: I am too small to go there.

TRAFFIKER: They give you good food. Chicken, coco cola.

COJO: Sir! I am only ten!

PHIL: Finally, the agent drives Cojo to the Ivory Coast.

COJO: Cojo was actually excited by how it will help his Mother.

PHIL: They avoided the border control.

COJO: Once across border, Cojo was completely alone.

PHIL: He was taken to a warehouse to sleep. The man who brought him disappeared.

COJO: There are many children in the warehouse, sometimes more than one hundred.

PHIL: The cocoa planters come and see the warehouse owner.

COJO: Then Cojo hears them negotiating his sale. He's taken to the plantation.

PHIL: One job was to transport the cocoa beans.

COJO: The bags were taller than him.

PHIL: People placed the bags onto Cojo's head.

COJO: They were so heavy he often fell down.

PHIL: The farmer beat him til he stood up to lift the bag.

COJO: These boys worked from six in the morning to about ten at night. We'd sit on the ground picking up cocoa pods with one hand and, with the other, hacking them open with machete to scoop out the beans.

PHIL: Common injury with machete was cutting…

COJO: … or accidental amputation *(Animate this with a horrifying scream)* on the hands.

PHIL: Open wounds expose the boys to HIV. Applying pesticides without the necessary protective equipment leads to horrific skin burns and respiratory damage…

PHIL & COJO: These can be fatal.

COJO: If they refuse to work, the plantation owners bring razors and slice their feet. They put salt in the wounds.

PHIL: The children have no communication with anyone.

COJO: One boy Cojo knew, tried to escape.

PHIL: The plantations are isolated, in the middle of forest. There are no roads out, just fields everywhere.

COJO: They tied my friend to a papaya tree. They beat him. They broke his arm.

PHIL: The pleasure that people from various nations around the world derive from chocolate could be at the expense of children trafficked and enslaved to harvest cocoa beans. Constantly hearing stories like these spurred us on in our work.

Silas Marner (2014)

MINISTER. SILAS. Serious.

Silas Marner *is my adaptation of George Eliot's classic book using verbatim techniques, i.e. all the words in the play derive from the Victorian novel, to capture accurately the feeling of the language.* ***Silas Marner****, a respectable weaver in 19th century England and a member of a strict religious community, is wrongly accused of theft and is forced to move to the faraway village of Raveloe. A robbery at his new home leaves Marner without his hard-earned gold and in the depths of depression. A mysterious, drug addicted woman is later found dead in the woods outside Marner's cottage. That same night he thinks his gold has returned... but it proves to be something very different...*

This scene is the accusation the Minister makes to Silas of the theft of some church money. It is important to know in the portrayal of Silas that he was innocent and was being set up by William Dane, who he thought was his friend. This should affect the way in which the scene is portrayed. The Minister is unaware of the set up... as far as we know! The characters are in the moment and emotions can and should run high! The original production was in the promenade style, with the action taking place amongst the audience. It would be an interesting idea to consider using this form of presentation in your performance. It makes the whole experience for your audience more immersive and visceral.

***

MINISTER:	*(Takes out a pocket knife.)* This is yours, Brother Marner?
SILAS:	Why yes. But...
MINISTER:	Where did you last have it?
SILAS:	I thought it were still in my pocket.
MINISTER:	I exhort you not to hide your sin. Confess and repent.
SILAS:	What is this? I have done nothing.
MINISTER:	You were in the bureau yesterday, tending our dear departed deacon were you not?

SILAS: I was.

MINISTER: The knife were found in the bureau where there also lain a bag of church money. Some hand removed that bag.

Pause.

SILAS: I know nothing about the knife being there, or the money being gone. Search me.

MINISTER: The proof is heavy against you, Brother Marner.

SILAS: Search my dwelling.

MINISTER: No man was there but you.

SILAS: I must have slept, or... or had another visitation. The thief must have come while I was not in the body. I say again, search me and my dwelling.

MINISTER: William Dane found the bag tucked behind the chest of drawers in your chamber... empty! *(He shows the bag.)*

SILAS: Have you ever known me to lie?

MINISTER: How do I know what you may do in the secret chambers of your heart to give Satan an advantage over you?

SILAS: I remember now. The knife wasn't in my pocket.

MINISTER: What mean you by these words?

SILAS: I shall say nothing more.

MINISTER: Speak out.

SILAS: I have no need. God will clear me.

MINISTER: The lots have declared you as Guilty. You are suspended from church membership. You must render up the stolen money.

SILAS: I do not have this money. God is my witness.

MINISTER: Brother Marner…

SILAS: *(Agitated but whispering.)* I never put the knife in my pocket. I took it out last to cut a strap for William. Why has he woven a plot to lay the sin at my door? I say he stole the money.

MINISTER: … to confess will be a sign of repentance. Only then may you be received back into the chapel.

SILAS: God is a God of lies, a God that bears witness against the innocent.

MINISTER: We can do nothing but pray for you, Silas.

Silas Marner (2)

SILAS. NARRATOR. Serious.

Silas Marner *is my adaptation of George Eliot's classic book, using verbatim techniques i.e. all the words in the play derive from the Victorian novel, to capture accurately the feeling of the language.* ***Silas Marner****, a respectable weaver in 19th century England and a member of a strict religious community, is wrongly accused of theft and is forced to move to the faraway village of Raveloe. A robbery at his new home leaves Marner without his hard-earned gold and in the depths of depression. A mysterious, drug addicted woman is later found dead in the woods outside Marner's cottage. That same night he thinks his gold has returned… but it proves to be something very different…*

This scene shows the moments leading to Silas' discovery of his own property being robbed. In the original play the narrator is voiced by an ensemble of actors, who I intended to add the feeling of Silas' panic from their manic movement on stage. In this two-person version, the Narrator needs to add movement that shows the way in which Silas' brain is racing. Silas' performance needs to be naturalistic and emotional. The narrator should be contrastingly stylistic. Remember, the Narrator can see and touch Silas, while Silas must remain unaware of their existence. This scene offers opportunities for lively, emotive, animated and imaginative performances. In this scene I decided to put the direct address in the third person (he/she rather than I/we). This aims to more clearly focus the audience's attention on the fact that the performers are not the real people in this scene. They become a commentator on the action and can, in the way they deliver the lines, 'comment' on them using facial expression or voice tone. The body of the performer can still exist in the time their narration is referring to (dual time performing) and when Silas speaks back in the real time he becomes first person (I/we) as he slips imperceptibly back into that time. Towards the end of the scene Silas could be said to be able to see the narrator and talk directly to him/her. The original production was in the promenade style, with the action taking place amongst the audience. It would be an interesting idea to consider using this form of presentation in your performance. It makes the whole experience for your audience more immersive and visceral.

***

SILAS: Marner reached his door satisfied his errand was done. To his short-sighted eyes everything was as he had left it. Once warm, he thought it pleasant to see his guineas on the table.

NARRATOR: Joy is the best of wine.

SILAS: Guineas were a golden wine. He placed his candle on the floor...

NARRATOR: ... near his loom.

SILAS: He swept away the sand...

NARRATOR: ... but noticed no change.

SILAS: He removed the bricks.

NARRATOR: The belief that his gold was gone could not come at once.

SILAS: 'Have my eyes deceived me?'

NARRATOR: He held the candle and examined the hole. He passed his trembling hands all about the hole.

SILAS: 'Did I put my gold somewhere else and forgotten where?'

NARRATOR: He searched every corner.

SILAS: Turned his bed over...

NARRATOR: ... shook it... kneaded it and when there was no other place to be searched...

SILAS: ... he kneeled down again and felt once more round the hole.

NARRATOR: There was no untried refuge left to shelter from the terrible truth. His gold was not there.

SILAS:	He put his trembling hands to his head.
NARRATOR:	He gave a cry of desolation.
SILAS:	'Noooooooo!'
NARRATOR:	The idea of a thief began to present itself.
SILAS:	*(Thinking aloud.)* 'A thief might be caught… and the gold restored!'
NARRATOR:	His thoughts glanced at neighbours, remarks or questions, now regarded as grounds for suspicion.
SILAS:	'Jem Rodney!'
NARRATOR:	… a known poacher…… disreputable.
SILAS:	'Jem's the man! He can be found and made to restore my money.'
NARRATOR:	Silas go and proclaim your loss.
SILAS:	'Squire Cass will make him deliver it up.'
NARRATOR:	Silas ran till want of breath compelled him to slacken his pace to the… Rainbow Pub.

*(**SILAS** makes the journey to the Rainbow pub.)*

SILAS:	*(Rushing in. Out of breath.)* 'Robbed! I've been robbed!'

Chequered Flags to Chequered Futures (2014)

ROY. CHRIS. Seriocomic.

Chequered Flags to Chequered Futures is my verbatim play telling of a car accident, which left each of the three occupants of one car with very different consequences. Chris was the backseat passenger in the car and suffered a very serious leg injury, leaving him physically disabled. Prior to the accident, Chris had become the World Champion Banger Racer, and this scene shows the beginning of that exciting journey as he tells his dad (Roy) that he has sold his model racing cars to buy and refurbish an old banger to race. The scene varies between 'live action' and reflective direct address speech. (Roy and Chris were wonderful in their interviews and spoke naturally quoting dialogue which was so helpful for me writing this verbatim play). Remember, with the direct address sections, it is important that the performers should meet the eyes of the audience (not just one person). This scene should have an exuberance and energy about it that, later in the play, is not possible. When words are in quotes it means Chris is quoting his thoughts. It is important to differentiate these lines by tone of voice and manner of movement. Try to convey Chris' cheekiness… that's important! The Victoria Shanghai Academy premiere of **Chequered Flags To Chequered Futures** *is available on the* **Chicken!** *DVD as a bonus feature.*

***

ROY: Chris then started to get into these model racing cars.

CHRIS: Yeh, I wanted to race something myself… little petrol engine ones with two speed gearboxes… quite impressive! The first time me 'n' Dad went to watch, it was quite funny 'cos you'd hear them going down the straights, and it was like *(Very high pitched.)* meeeeeee *(Slightly less high-pitched.)* meeeeeee … and we'd go,

CHRIS & ROY: Are they changing gear?

ROY: These little cars… were like a thousand quid each! It was big money!

CHRIS: We went to Staffordshire thinking we had the nuts of a setup. The world champion was there and they are… they're professionals… you know… you think what you've got is good, then you look at theirs and you think "we're nothing!" They'd be spending tens of thousands! Just randomly through work, one of my friends started racing, you know, real cars at Matchams. I'd just passed my driving test so I said "I'll come and watch." ... and I thought... "Yeh. That's do-able"...

... not really knowing... you know... not really knowing about how much you could pick a car up for... so I got home, and... well, we had a great big row about it!

ROY: Don't be so bloody daft! It'll cost too much!

CHRIS: You can pick them up for nothing.

ROY: You don't know enough about them. You'll have to buy a race seat, decent crash helmet, harness, rolling cage, window nets. Where are you gonna get the money from? What happens if you crash?

CHRIS: To be quite truthful Dad, I've already got the car. I'm picking it up in a couple of weeks.

ROY: Where you got the money from?

CHRIS: Sold all my radio-controlled car stuff.

ROY: What?

CHRIS: Yeh.

ROY: It's not just racing them. You got to get the suspension tweaked, you don't know nothing about that!

CHRIS: Well, I'll learn.

I'd proper got the bit for this so I'd already arranged for someone to come round and buy all my gear. I didn't sell it for what it was worth... just what it'd cost me to start up racing. I also got a cheap trailer and took the car over to my dad's workshop. He was looking round it and was like:

ROY: Smart!

CHRIS: ... and he ended up...

ROY: I could do this!

CHRIS: *(Laughing)* Within a week he'd bought a car!

ROY: Of course it really did get Chris and me close, I can see that. None of my other lads wanted to know… his brothers, you know, they weren't interested and he was just getting better and better…

CHRIS & ROY: *(Laughing.)* …and winning as well!

I Love You, Mum – I Promise I Won't Die (2016)

FIONA. TIM. Serious.

*This is taken from **I Love You, Mum – I Promise I Won't Die**, my verbatim play telling the tragic story of Daniel Spargo-Mabbs, who died as a result of a drug overdose he took at an illegal rave. The words are verbatim. Tim and Fiona (Dan's parents) describe the heartbreaking hours that led to Daniel's death. I have added an additional speech to the end of this scene, Tim and Fiona's reflections on his passing which, in the original play, come later. These speeches are delivered as a direct address but the two people can and should relate to each other as well, to show they are telling this story to the audience together with shared memories. I suggest they look at the one who is talking whenever they are not. As a performer, when addressing the audience, you should meet the eyes of the audience (not just one person). Do not fix your eyes above their heads. It needs to be personal and 'direct'. The words become a narrative 'voice over' as though in the present, looking back, while you re-live (it may not take much action in this scene) the events in the scene, offering the audience a heartfelt representation of the memories. OYT's production of **I Love You, Mum – I Promise I Won't Die** is available on DVD via Salamander Street.*

***

FIONA: At 5:30 on Monday morning. I was texting people, saying: 'He's nearly through the twelve hours and he's still with us.'
I just thought, 'If he can keep going then his heart would get stronger and work by itself'… but, when they did handovers after 8:30 the consultant came out and said there was no surgical option. They… they'd got no choice. I was saying: 'I don't want to have to make the decision.' And the consultant said:

TIM: There is no decision to make.

FIONA: They were gonna have to switch… (**FIONA** *finds it too hard to finish the sentence.*)

TIM: All hope had gone. I received the news coldly and quietly.

The image of vultures returned, one perched on each shoulder, pushing me to the floor.

I'll never forget walking towards the toilet and repeating over and over in my head: 'He's gonna die. He's really gonna die. My son is going to die.' It was as if someone had invented a new colour, for which language didn't yet exist, and words were just sucked into it and disappeared.

FIONA: *(Very much more together.)* My parents had come up from Swanage, in Dorset. They got an earlier train than planned and, thankfully, made it before he died.

We were all there, stood around his bed. There was something incredibly peaceful about... about his dying. It was just... it shouldn't have been but it was.

TIM: Yeah.

FIONA: A nurse talked us through what would happen. I was just holding his face and whispering in his ear, saying: 'It's okay Dan. I love you <u>so</u> much but now it's time for you to go... to go and be with Jesus.'
I remember what it felt like. It's really hard to be back there. It took just twenty minutes for him to die. I couldn't let go of his face after the beeps did the continual beep. I knew when I did, he would go cold, and never be warm again. I held him for what seemed like ages but I... I had to let go.

TIM: Dan put himself beyond our reach in a number of ways, particularly now we know he'd done this before and covered it up so well. I'm very sad because we had protections in place for good reasons but he managed to get round them. They were there for his good.

FIONA: When people talk about having an aching or broken heart, I'd always assumed this was metaphorical. I didn't know it'd be an actual, physical pain. From the first moment you know you're expecting a child, your identity, energies and focus are on that new little being. A massive part of who you then are, is being that person's mum, pouring an infinite quantity of love into them. I still have all that for Dan, but I don't know what I do with it. I don't know who I am now... now I can't be Daniel's mum.

Scratching the Surface (2016)

MARK WHEELLER. TEENAGER. Serious.

Scratching the Surface is my verbatim play about self-harm. It has two distinct strands. Firstly, the story of a family of a teenager, who self-harmed while at school but stopped after leaving. They talk openly about it. Secondly, a drama group in the Midlands, who I interviewed to establish what they knew about the subject of self-harm. My task was to weave the two interview strands together. This is a section where I (Mark), interview the drama group. One of the group opens up and reveals a background story he had experienced. It took a lot of courage, was totally unexpected and there was some tension in the air as the person knew the words could be (and were) used in the play. The speech is a verbatim account but, aside from the first line, does not need to be delivered by direct address. You must decide whether to present this scene as it is (with two people sitting down and simply talking) or (preferably) add something more interesting/stylistic/symbolic to bring it alive. How can you convey the relationship between the two people? It is an unusual one. The Teenager needs to find ways to differentiate between the voices in the speech (voice in head and Mum) and I suggest opportunities for movement need to be sought out. Alderbrook School's production of Scratching the Surface is available on DVD via Salamander Street.

***

MARK: I'd asked Rob if he'd ever thought of suicide? Other than saying he had, he didn't want to elaborate but when it came up with the drama group, and this is the absolute truth… one lad suddenly said, with no real warning…

TEENAGER: I've had one family member die because of depression… and self-harm.

MARK: Suicide?

TEENAGER: I… they couldn't cope. Then, I've also had someone who's shown me that if you speak to someone, you can get through. I've got a very, very close friend who self-harms and I just felt, like, everything built up inside and I just needed to release it. So, I broke one of the razors *(Long*

pause to gather thoughts and hold back emotions.) I went down the
bottom of the garden... *(Long pause, blows nose.)* ... and I
kind of felt better.

MARK: They were being incredibly open. I said: 'I wasn't
expecting any of this. I... I'm really amazed that this is
something you all seem to relate to so closely.' So, where
did you cut yourself?

TEENAGER: Like, on my side and my leg. It made me feel better and
then the next day I just felt really bad again.

MARK: I'm really sorry to keep asking questions...

TEENAGER: It's alright.

MARK: ... but **how** did it make you feel better and for how long?

TEENAGER: I was shaking when I did it. It just helped me cos now
I know what they'd gone through and I needed to try
harder with them.

MARK: How long ago was this?

TEENAGER: About a year ago.

MARK: So where are you now and is this ever...?

TEENAGER: Never gonna happen again.

MARK: It's never gonna happen again?

TEENAGER: No, no.

MARK: You say that very definitely.

TEENAGER: Yeh.

MARK: Because?

TEENAGER: It took me to a really bad place.

MARK: Right.

TEENAGER: It'll never happen again.

MARK: How did you get out of that really bad place?

TEENAGER: I spoke to my mum.

MARK: Brave.

TEENAGER: I just said: 'Mum, I don't feel right.' And then, she spoke to me and I spoke to my girlfriend and it… it helped.

MARK: One of the group said to me: 'People who self-harm feel like there is no one they can speak to. Speaking to or even listening to someone who's done it is more likely to help you get over it.' Then I said:
Is there anything you want to say…

TEENAGER: We are a generation that wants to be liked. When you see that 'like' on your photo you think, 'Oh my God I'm, I'm being liked', but there's all this negative energy as well. So just as easily you can feel you're nothing… not worth being here almost… not loved and alone in the world. That's hard. I'm glad to be tackling this head on because, most of the time, the person doing the self-harm isn't the reason for the self-harm. Sometimes it's people being demoralising or mean to them… like from family, or peers. Sometimes it's bullying. Whatever the reason it needs tackling.

MARK: Well, I'll just finish off by saying that this experience of talking to you has been remarkable for me. I had no idea there was this kind of… erm… passion behind this topic.

This Is For You (2017)

JOHN. IAN. Set in 1974. Seriocomic.

This Is For You *is an immersive, site-specific (café – we decked our drama studio out as a café) play, co-written by Matt Beames. It tells two stories. The first, set in the 1970s, tells of an unplanned teenage pregnancy. The second, set in 2016, sees the surviving characters being forced to deal with the fallout from their past. It features, as a backdrop, the music of Mick Ronson, who was the iconic guitarist in one of David Bowie's early bands,* ***The Spiders From Mars****. Both Susan and John were written as Mick Ronson fans (as am I).* ***This Is For You*** *was conceived as a radio play and then became an immersive play set in a cafe, with the audience being the customers. It may be an interesting idea to play with where the audience are if you choose to present this scene. In the original performance it was set in one corner of the 'café' with Ian lying on a bed (coffee table covered for this scene by a duvet) with John entering from the opposite diagonal, walking past the audience as he approaches Ian. This is the opening scene, set up to establish the sibling relationship between Ian and John. The characters are 'in the moment' in this scene. Be sure to note the higher status of Ian, who holds the power in this scene as he has money!*

The original OYT production of ***This Is For You*** *is available to watch on YouTube.*

***

JOHN: Ian!

The plays as though through headphones. **IAN** *is reading the album cover of* ***The Lamb Lies Down on Broadway*** *and has period headphones on. John enters in an excited manner.*

Ian! *(Pulling* **IAN***'s headphones off.)* Ian!

IAN: What? *(He removes the headphones and the sound of the headphone music stops.)*

JOHN: She said yes!

IAN: Who did?

JOHN: Suzi.

IAN:	Baytes?
JOHN:	Yeah.
IAN:	Said yes to what?
JOHN:	To going out with me!
IAN:	You?
JOHN:	Gee, thanks!
IAN:	No, I mean, Suzi's lovely… but… well…
JOHN:	What?
IAN:	You're hardly the Six Million Dollar Man are you?
JOHN:	Mick Ronson.
IAN:	You're not even him!
JOHN:	No, I mean… he's at the Rainbow in April, so I asked her… but… there's a problem.
IAN:	Tickets pricey are they?
JOHN:	Yeh.
IAN:	What'll you do then?
JOHN:	You lend me it? Your birthday money? I'll give it back on Saturday when I get paid. It's just that… they might sell out.
IAN:	Doubt it!
JOHN:	Bowie sold out really fast.
IAN:	He's not Bowie! It'd be like Phil Collins going solo…

JOHN: Who?

IAN: Genesis' drummer.

JOHN: *(Laughing.)* Ronson will be really big… you'll see.

IAN: Will he?

JOHN: Yes. Now please Ian… can I borrow the money?

IAN: How much?

JOHN: £2.50 each.

IAN: That's five quid John!

JOHN: Brothers are supposed to help each other.

IAN: What do I get out of it?

JOHN: I've got two quid so I only need three… and I will pay you back on Saturday. *(IAN's reaction elicits the next words.)* With a bit of interest?

IAN: Now this sounds much more interesting. A fiver on Saturday and it's a deal?

JOHN: For three quid?

IAN: Yeah.

JOHN: Four.

IAN: Five.

JOHN: I only get paid five fifty!

IAN: *(Getting the money out of his pocket and smiling broadly.)* You'll have 50 new pence change then!

JOHN: Brothers are meant to help each other!

IAN: I am. *(**IAN** holds three pound notes in the air.)*

JOHN: *(Takes it after a moment's thought.)* Bastard Ian! *(**IAN** laughs.)*

IAN: Don't let Dad hear you using that language!

JOHN: Wanker! *(**IAN** laughs. Pause.)*

IAN: Just pay me back on Saturday.

JOHN *exits leaving* **IAN** *on stage putting his headphones back on, chuckling to himself.*
The Lamb Lies Down on Broadway *fades back up.*

This Is For You (2)

IAN. SUZI. Set in 1974. Serious.

This Is For You *is an immersive, site-specific (café – we decked our drama studio out as a café) play, co-written by Matt Beames. It tells two stories. The first, set in the 1970s, tells of an unplanned teenage pregnancy. The second, set in 2016, sees the surviving characters being forced to deal with the fallout from their past. It features, as a backdrop, the music of Mick Ronson, who was the iconic guitarist in one of David Bowie's early bands,* ***The Spiders From Mars***. *Both Susan and John were written as Mick Ronson fans (as am I).* ***This Is For You*** *was originally conceived as a radio play but became an immersive play set in a cafe, with the audience being the customers. It would be interesting to play with where the audience are if you choose to present this scene. In the original performance, this scene was delivered in the middle of the 'cafe' with the audience all around. This is the scene where a huge twist (that is further twisted later on) is revealed. Suzi has fallen pregnant, unplanned at the age of fifteen. John is the father. This is a few days after they first discovered the news. John must arrive in the scene out of breath… genuinely out of breath. This will affect his delivery of the lines. Suzi is there to tell him something that will affect the rest of their lives. It is a huge scene emotionally. (I should tell you that what Suzi tells John is actually a lie, on the instruction of her all-powerful father. This should affect the approach the performer of Suzi has to the motivation regarding the delivery of the lines. John has no idea that what she says is a lie. If you can avoid the performer playing John, knowing this (somehow by covering up what is written here) it might help. After the performance you can have fun explaining it to the performer!).*
Note the symbolic nature of the prop (record). It appears later in the play so becomes hugely significant. The characters are both 'in the moment' in this scene. The original OYT production of ***This Is For You*** *is available to watch on YouTube.*

***

A park: **SUZI** *enters carrying an LP record* ***(Slaughter)*** *in a bag. The sound of a park in the summer.* **JOHN** *enters running, towards* **SUZI**. *When he speaks at first he is out of breath.*

SUZI: Where've you been?

JOHN: Sorry Suz. Work kept me.

SUZI:	This mattered!
JOHN:	I couldn't help it, honest! Sorry.
SUZI:	We're moving.
JOHN:	What?
SUZI:	Mum and Dad are moving up north.
JOHN:	With you?
SUZI:	Yeah.
JOHN:	Because? Where?
SUZI:	Macclesfield. Near Manchester.
JOHN:	Manchester?
SUZI:	My dad didn't want me to see you, so that's what he's decided to do. He thinks I'm at Janet's now. Mum dropped me off here to say goodbye to you so I can't stay long. My God, if he finds out…
JOHN:	When're you going?
SUZI:	This weekend. He's already sorted a job for himself! We're gonna live at his brother's.
JOHN:	He's got everything all worked out then.
SUZI:	You have no idea!
JOHN:	There must be something we can do?
SUZI:	There isn't! Whatever you, do we'll be moving. Whatever anyone does. It's decided John.

JOHN: I'll tell my mum and dad. I said I would once you'd…

SUZI: …there's nothing to tell.

JOHN: What?

Silence.

Suzi?

SUZI: It's been 'taken care of' as my mum puts it.

A moment, then realisation hits.

JOHN: You mean…?

SUZI: That's where I was on Tuesday. Mum took me in and… they were really worried about how it'd look for your dad.

JOHN: My dad?

SUZI: Yeah.

JOHN: but this is the last thing he'd want. Killing… ah…

SUZI: It's too late.

JOHN: You cannot make him the reason for…

SUZI: I told you. My dad decided!

JOHN: He had no right.

SUZI: *(Laughs.)* He doesn't worry about rights.

JOHN: But you didn't talk to me.

SUZI: He went completely mental… it was horrible.

JOHN: Why didn't you talk to me?

SUZI:	I couldn't.
JOHN:	You could. You could've phoned… you could have…
SUZI:	There's nothing you can do! Nothing!
JOHN:	I could have told you what I thought… could have told you what my dad would think. I know he wouldn't want to be an excuse for this!
SUZI:	I thought you'd be grateful. We had to…
JOHN:	Grateful?
SUZI:	Maybe it's best that we are moving, 'cos you don't understand.
JOHN:	Suz…
SUZI:	No one can ever know about this… No one! Promise me, John. No one! (**JOHN** *makes to hug her and* **SUSAN** *pushes him away.*) I need you to promise me.
JOHN:	*(Struggling, despite the directness of what he says.)* Of course I won't.
SUZI:	Promise me!
JOHN:	I promise.
SUZI:	Dad's said I can't see or contact you at all… ever!
JOHN:	What?
SUZI:	'Fresh start.' That's what he's says.
	Pause.
JOHN:	Suzi, just…

SUZI:	I have to go, I'm sorry.
JOHN:	You can't!
SUZI:	He'll be waiting. Look, I want to give you this but I don't want a big…
JOHN:	What is it?
SUZI:	Slaughter.
JOHN:	I've already got it.
SUZI:	This one is special.

She hands him her autographed copy of 'Slaughter on 10th Avenue'.

JOHN:	Suzi…
SUZI:	I want you to have something you know means **a lot** to me. I want you to be clear about how I felt about you. I'm so sorry it's ended like this. It's really not my fault. *(Her voice is breaking and she may become tearful, so turns to avoid eye contact.)* I will remember you, I want you to know that, and…
JOHN:	… and what?
SUZI:	I'll remember you forever John. All of my life. Look after it please.

She kisses him on the cheek and leaves. He tries to hold her but she pulls away. **JOHN** *remains in shock.*

Can You Hear Me Major Tom? (2019)

WENDY. JUNE. Seriocomic.

*This is taken from **Can You Hear Me Major Tom?**, a fan tribute
(documentary) play developed in the aftermath of the sudden and unexpected death of
David Bowie.*
*Wendy is an avid David Bowie fan. The scene (and the play) are about the nature
of being a fan, so if you have difficulty relating to the specifics, imagine your reaction
to something/someone who you idolise. Wendy is passionate about her commitment to
David Bowie and Woody Woodmansey (David Bowie's **Spiders From Mars**
and the **Holy Holy** drummer). The opening speech narrates into the scene and is
delivered as a direct address. As such, it is important that you should meet the eyes of
the audience (not just one person). Do not fix your eyes above their heads. It needs to be
personal and 'direct'. The remainder of the scene is a re-enactment of a conversation
Wendy remembers clearly. The scene leads to the excitement of her actually meeting
Woody Woodmansey. June is Woody's wife and shows her amusement at Wendy's
reaction… because to her, Woody is just a bloke, her husband. I should add that June
and Wendy have since become friends, so there was obviously some positive chemistry
between them!*

***

WENDY: David Bowie has been the soundtrack to my life. He saw
me through school. I was bullied for being a Bowie fan but
he taught me to be individual.

In 2013, the sole remaining **Spider from Mars**, Woody
Woodmansey, announced that he was reuniting with
David's bass player and longtime producer, Tony Visconti
to tour **The Man Who Sold The World** with their band
Holy Holy and David's blessing. Did I go? You bet I did!
I arrived at Peckham Junction Station and asked directions
from a random lady:

JUNE: The Holy Holy gig?

WENDY: Yeh. You going?

JUNE:	*(Smiling.)* Yeh, and the one tomorrow.
WENDY:	Same.
JUNE:	I have an excuse. I'm the drummer's wife.
WENDY:	Woody?
JUNE:	Yeh.
WENDY:	You're not?
JUNE:	I am!
WENDY:	June Woodmansey?
JUNE:	*(Laughing.)* You know my name. That's so funny!
WENDY:	Do you mind if I walk with you?
JUNE:	Course not.
WENDY:	This is so weird. I've been a fan since... well the...
JUNE:	The Spiders?
WENDY:	Yeh.
JUNE:	I'll introduce you to Woody?
WENDY:	'Oh my god!' We laugh at that now. I told her about my brother and how he met them when he was... and that he died... She phoned him and Woody Woodmansey came out to meet us. 'I can't believe this!' And then Woody Woodmansey hugged ME!

I cried and felt reconnected with John, my brother, who had met Bowie back in the day but who had died when I was very young. In 2015, I helped on the Holy Holy merchandise stand on their UK tour. Seeing the private side of these guys, my love and respect was multiplied. *(She pulls out a copy of the live album.)* When the live album came out, my name was on it for doing the merchandise stall.

Game Over (2019)

OLLIE. MATT. Serious.

*This is taken from **Game Over**, my verbatim play telling of Breck Bednar's murder by an online predator, Lewis Daynes (LD). Ollie and Matt are Breck's friends, both online and in real life. This scene amalgamates a few from the play to make this extract. It is a verbatim account Ollie and Matt gave me (separately) over the phone. It shows a key point of the play where the two boys (on the same server as Breck) begin to suspect that LD is not what he pretends to be. They explain this to the audience, so the audience are aware, while Breck's mum has only her suspicions to confront Breck with. It's an example of dramatic irony (the audience knowing something someone on stage isn't aware of). The scene could be staged seated at tables with computer screens or in Zoom style windows.*

The separate speeches are delivered as a direct address but (unless presenting it Zoom style) may also involve looking at the other person when they are talking. When speaking to the audience it is important that you catch the eyes of the audience as well. Do not fix your eyes above their heads. It needs to be 'direct'. When LD speaks I have allocated the lines as a unison presentation by both Ollie and Matt. There should be something different about their delivery of LD's lines to reflect the sinister nature of his character. The final line is not an LD line although I have allocated here as a unison line. Both lads were thinking the same thought.

***

OLLIE: Lewis Daynes ran a TeamSpeak server and er, seemed like a… like a nice lad…

MATT: … welcoming, keen to build up a community of like-minded people.

OLLIE: I was the first person in the gang to meet Lewis, a year before I met Breck, so I kind of feel responsible for what happened because, you know, I introduced them.

MATT: He'd pop on to say…

OLLIE/MATT: *(As **LD**.)* Hello. How you all doing?

MATT: We were all in awe of his technical ability. He even bought us a game or two!

OLLIE: After a while, I asked him if he'd set up a TeamSpeak server for my friends. He did and gradually it started expanding. By the time Breck joined us, we were a quite large group, around fifteen, most of us living in Caterham.

MATT: I first spoke to Breck, playing Minecraft.

OLLIE: Soon we met up…

MATT: … and just sort of hung out for a bit. Breck was into Battlefield 3 and, 'cos he spent more time playing than us, he was much, much better despite me being the year above him at school.

OLLIE: I knew Breck was in the Redhill Air Cadets and he urged me to join, so I spoke to him there as well. Lewis told me he was a defence contractor, with work and important meetings in Washington.

MATT: Lewis gradually became Breck's mentor, and he soaked up information for a career he wanted desperately.

OLLIE: I've met and made good friends through gaming and then, from that, I'd Skype them, see their faces, hear their parents, their brothers and sisters, so I know they're just another teenager sitting at their computer, chilling, playing games.

MATT: Unbeknown to Breck's mum, Ollie, and some of us older ones, were beginning to suspect Lewis Daynes wasn't all that he made himself out to be.

OLLIE: I mean, I was going to an air show. I went every year with friends, some who I'd met over the internet. It was safe, in a public place and I asked Lewis if he wanted to join us. He declined:

OLLIE/MATT: *(As **LD**.)* I'm busy with work…

MATT: Every time we planned something, he'd be like:

OLLIE/MATT: *(As **LD**.)* I can't do that, I'm in America.

OLLIE: … or

OLLIE/MATT: *(As **LD**.)* I'm seeing family.

OLLIE: Then, when we'd Skype, he didn't have a webcam. That was odd.

LD: It's not working.
OLLIE: ... or...

OLLIE/MATT: *(As LD.)* I've been so busy I haven't ordered a new one yet.

OLLIE: It just kept happening.

MATT: We asked him to send photos and he sent fake ones.

OLLIE: One time he told me he had to get a flight back from Washington on a large military aircraft and they had a problem over the Atlantic, so they made an emergency landing on an aircraft carrier. Now, me being a massive aviation geek, I just knew that was physically impossible. It was a flat out lie. 'We'd've heard about it on the news though, Lewis!'

OLLIE/MATT: *(As LD.)* No, no no! 'cos it'd be such an embarrassment to the government!

OLLIE: I just thought, that's bollocks! Maybe he's doing it so we like him more or to seem... like a cooler person.
Then we started to think...

OLLIE/MATT: ... mmm, maybe you're not a defence contractor either?

Salamander Street

Teachers – if you are interested in buying a set of texts for your class please email info@salamanderstreet.com – we would be happy to discuss discounts and keep you up to date with our latest publications and study guides.

Act Normal:
Contemporary Monologues by Mark Wheeller
Paperback 9781913630607
eBook 9781913630591

Salamander Street will be publishing new editions of Mark's plays in 2020 – follow us on Twitter or Facebook or visit our website for the latest news.

www.ingramcontent.com/pod-product-compliance
Lightning Source LLC
Jackson TN
JSHW080205141224
75386JS00029B/1045